I0815539

Living by God's Unshakable Promises

JESUS EVERY DAY

JIM CYMBALA

with Rebecca English Lawson

A Tyndale nonfiction imprint

Visit Tyndale online at tyndale.com.

Visit Tyndale Momentum online at tyndalemomentum.com.

Visit the author at http://jimcymbala.org.

Tyndale, Tyndale's quill logo, *Tyndale Momentum*, and the Tyndale Momentum logo are registered trademarks of Tyndale House Ministries. Tyndale Momentum is a nonfiction imprint of Tyndale House Publishers, Carol Stream, Illinois.

Jesus Every Day: Living by God's Unshakable Promises

Cover photograph of metal leaves by Evie S. on Unsplash.com.

Author photograph provided by author and used with permission. All rights reserved.

Interior illustrations of leaves and borders by Rawpixel.

Cover design by Faceout Studio, Jeff Miller.

Interior design by Laura Cruise.

Published in association with the literary agencies of Ann Spangler & Company and Tom Dean, Literary Agent with A Drop of Ink LLC, www.adropofink.pub.

All emphases in Scripture quotations have been added by the author.

For information about special discounts for bulk purchases, please contact Tyndale House Publishers at csresponse@tyndale.com, or call 1-855-277-9400.

ISBN 979-8-4005-0607-9

Printed in China

31 30 29 28 27 26 25
7 6 5 4 3 2 1

To my three children,
Chrissy, Sue, and James,
who have learned the secret of
walking daily with Jesus Christ

INTRODUCTION

When the Lord called me into the ministry, I had no formal training. I had a degree in sociology with a minor in philosophy, but I had really gone to college to play basketball. So books became my professors. I began to read and study so that I could minister effectively.

Along with commentaries on books of the Bible and Hebrew and Greek grammar studies, I started collecting devotionals. The writings of people like D. L. Moody, A. B. Simpson, and Lettie Cowman, who compiled the classic devotional *Streams in the Desert*, encouraged my heart and helped me draw closer to Jesus.

I developed a habit of reading from several different devotionals every morning, which I still do today. Each day I read the devotions for that day's date. I note the verse chosen for each of the entries, and then I read the entire chapter in the Bible where each of those verses is found. This pushes me all around the Bible, so I'm not focused in just one place. It leads to various thoughts that the Lord makes real to my heart. I so appreciate devotionals.

Some of the ones I've read have strong Bible content but use archaic English that's hard for many of us today to understand. Some of the newer ones I've read are not so spiritually meaty. So when I was asked to write this one-hundred-day devotional, I tried to write one that was both biblically substantive but was also in my own voice so that it would be easy to understand.

As I mention several times throughout this book, a devotional isn't meant to replace our time in God's Word and with the Lord in prayer. Instead, it should encourage us, inspire us, and make us more hungry to be with Jesus every day and to be strengthened by God's unshakable promises. That is why I'm writing this book—not that my thought for each day is sufficient on its own, but I want it to be an arrow pointing us to spend time with Christ.

Let's be encouraged by the devotionals we read, including this one, but let's also allow them to draw us nearer to the Lord Jesus every day so that our lives can be truly changed by his Holy Spirit teaching us, which makes us mature in him.

1

SMALL BEGINNINGS

Who dares despise the day of small things?

ZECHARIAH 4:10, NIV

When I came to pastor the Brooklyn Tabernacle decades ago, we had just a handful of people. At first I had natural enthusiasm. I wasn't seminary trained, and my sermons were bad, and the offerings were pitiful—the first one I collected was eighty-five dollars—but I still felt that God had called me.

One Tuesday night, I was getting ready for our evening meeting, which always had a meager turnout. I came downstairs from my little office (which was so small that when I counseled couples, it could hold only me and one other person at a time!). When I walked into the sanctuary, I saw two women. Not two thousand. Not two hundred. Not even fifteen or twenty, like we sometimes had on a Sunday. Two. My heart sank.

Zerubbabel, an Old Testament leader, battled discouragement too. Israel had been in captivity for seventy years in Babylon. But now God had Zerubbabel and a dedicated remnant of people return to resettle the land they had been driven from. Their first priority was to rebuild the Temple. So on the spot where Solomon's Temple had stood before being destroyed by the invading Babylonians, they started to work.

Many of the younger people shouted for joy. But most of the older ones remembered the glory of the former Temple, and when they saw the new foundation, they "wept aloud" (Ezra 3:12). *My goodness,* they thought. *After what we once had, you're going to call this the new Temple? I mean, really.* It was almost an embarrassment.

But God encouraged Zerubbabel and the people: "Zerubbabel's hands have laid the foundation of this Temple, and his hands will complete it. Who dares despise the day of small things?" (see Zechariah 4:9-10).

When we build or rebuild, things always start small. Maybe you've stepped out to serve the Lord in some new way, and the fire is barely alive, with just a few embers glowing. Maybe you've witnessed to neighbors and not much seems to be happening. That's when the enemy whispers, "Nothing is going to come of this!"

When I saw those two ladies that night, I took the microphone, trying to act like a polished preacher. I should have said, "Hey, sisters, would you just come up here and pray and wait on God with me?" Afterward, I felt so defeated. How I needed God to encourage me. And he did. He spoke to my heart, "Two is better than one—better than *none*. Don't despise the day of small things."

Everybody wants to be successful overnight. We all want to see our entire neighborhood come to Christ, but our next-door neighbor won't even open his door. The enemy laughs. "Ha, he'll never turn to God. Give it up!"

Let's never despise the day of small things. What God begins, he will finish. He will honor our work for him and turn it into something beautiful for his glory. We will be able to praise him and then help others who are ready to quit. It's always too soon to quit! Let's trust God. He will bring his purpose to pass as we walk with him day by day.

Lord, I believe that you are with me, but it's discouraging when I don't see much fruit. Help me to stay faithful, trusting that you are up to something great for your glory.

2

HAVE YOU ASKED GOD?

David asked the L*ORD*, *"Should I go out to fight the Philistines?"*

2 SAMUEL 5:19

"We're moving to Pennsylvania," someone told me. "They have something called green grass there. My family has got to get out of the hood." They had no thought of what church to attend, no thought of God's will for their lives. The story did not end well. Oh, the heartache I've encountered from people who ended up in situations they never imagined because they didn't inquire of the Lord.

When David became king of Israel, the Philistines, who were enemies of God, went in full force to knock him out before he could gain momentum. When he found out they were coming, David could have said, "Let's get the people with the most experience in military operations." Now there's a time for counsel, but that's not what David needed.

He could have said, as some do today, "Wait a minute. I'm a child of Abraham and God's anointed one. That means every place I go, I automatically have victory." That's wrong. God's choosing us does not guarantee his support if we're operating outside his will for our lives.

David was so dependent on God, so childlike in his faith, that he inquired, "Lord, what do I do? Should I fight them? Will you give us the victory?" The same God he had trusted when wrestling lions and bears as a shepherd boy and when facing the giant Goliath, he now trusted as king. That was the secret of David's strength.

The Lord answered David, "Go. I will deliver them into your hand." David fought the battle, and he won.

Then the Philistines attacked again. David could have said, "I did it once; I'll do it again." Instead, he sought direction from the Lord again, and God told him, "Do not go straight up, but circle around behind them" (2 Samuel 5:23, NIV). God doesn't necessarily lead the same way twice. We need to say, like David, "I've got to be sure that God is directing me." Only then can we be confident of victory.

Too many of us make decisions without consulting the Lord.

"I'm leaving my job. This other one pays more."

That's true, but does God want you there? Sometimes more is less.

"I'm gonna marry him. I'm getting older, and I don't want to be a spinster."

But did you pray about that? Are you spiritually compatible? Is this God's will for your life?

Other people, when they hear about the Holy Spirit's leading, say, "That's supernatural mysticism. I just read the Word." But the Word does not have specific answers for many questions we face in life. The Bible teaches us to marry a fellow believer, but it doesn't say which one. And there are a lot of single Christians out there to choose from.

How we need to be more like David in making decisions. When God sees that we want to be directed by him and to do things his way, oh, how that pleases him! Let's come to God as little children and not take a step without him going before us.

Lord, I don't want to make my own plans.
I want yours. Help me to be like David,
depending on you in childlike faith for every
decision. Then I can be sure that you will
be with me and will add your blessing.

3

A BROKEN SPIRIT

The sacrifice you desire is a broken spirit.
You will not reject a broken and repentant heart, O God.

PSALM 51:17

King David had committed adultery with Bathsheba, and to cover it up, he had her husband, Uriah, murdered. So God sent the prophet Nathan to the king with a strong message: "You're the man! You have sinned before God." Immediately David, out of deep guilt and brokenness, said, "Have mercy on me, O God" (Psalm 51:1). He didn't justify his evil actions; he admitted the truth: "God, I'm wrong. It's not my background; it's not my environment; it's not someone else's fault. I messed up."

Then David, although living in Old Testament times, foresaw the coming of the age of grace. He prayed, "You don't want animal sacrifices" (see Psalm 51:16). Now throughout the Old Testament, God had said, "You must offer the blood of animals as atonement for your sin." But David saw ahead to something deeper. He realized that people could offer sacrifices mechanically, by rote. In fact, that became the problem with Israel. They were sacrificing at the Temple but living apart from God, just like many today who go to church every Sunday but are living far from Jesus.

David said, "God, I know what you're really after. My sacrifice will be a broken spirit, a broken and contrite heart. As long as I protect my self-life and make excuses or blame others, the animal sacrifices are worthless."

I had been at the Brooklyn Tabernacle for a few months, and the church was going nowhere. I was trying to lead, but I was failing. I was trying to act like the preachers I had seen growing up. I wore a facade because of my insecurity and pride.

One day, alone in the sanctuary on a Tuesday afternoon in our run-down building, knowing that there wouldn't be even ten people in the service that night, I paced back and forth, saying, "God, you have to change this church." I had inherited some beautiful people, but others were divisive. I complained, "There's no money, the building's falling apart, the roof leaks. Oh, God, why did you put me in downtown Brooklyn with problems all around me?"

Out of nowhere, I sensed the Holy Spirit say, "I'll tell you the main problem in this church: It's you. You're prayerless. You're not sincere. You just want to get through the service some way, somehow. Your sermons aren't coming from things I am revealing to you in the Word. You don't really care about the people. *You're the problem.*"

I fell to my knees and wept. I knew it was true. Were there other real problems? Were there members who possibly weren't even Christians? Yes. But the main problem was me. To the glory of God, when I let the Lord break me, my preaching got better, my study of the Bible improved, and my prayer life increased.

When God gives us broken and contrite hearts, we are able to see the truth. It can hurt a bit, but he lovingly tells us what's wrong so he can make us right.

Lord, forgive us for protecting our self-life rather than surrendering ourselves to you. We can do nothing without you. Remind us to keep our eyes on you all day and every day.

4

THE TOUCH OF JESUS

He laid his right hand on me and said, "Don't be afraid!"

REVELATION 1:17

I was preaching in a foreign country and having a bit of a struggle. I couldn't tell if it was the indifference of the crowd or spiritual opposition or something else, but I was finding it hard going.

The prayer band at the Brooklyn Tabernacle knows my schedule, whether I'm in California or Florida or Haiti. Even when there's a time difference, they know exactly when I'm ministering, and they are praying. As I struggled to speak that day, suddenly an infusion of spiritual energy, faith, fervency, and words was given to me. I kept ministering, but I wondered, *Oh, God, what is happening right now?* In that moment I sensed the Lord saying to me, "Someone is praying for you." And in answer to that prayer, he touched me.

When the apostle John was exiled to the isle of Patmos, he experienced a glorious revelation of the risen Christ, which was overwhelming. In fact, it was too much for him, and he fell at Jesus' feet as though dead. But Jesus placed his right hand on John and said, "Don't be afraid!" (Revelation 1:17). In that instant everything changed. John was given strength to write the words of Christ and carry out God's purpose for him.

That is not the only time the touch of Jesus changed everything. When Jesus put his hands on a leper, the man's leprosy disappeared.

When Jesus laid his hands on the eyes of a blind man, the man's sight was restored. When Jesus touched the children, they were blessed.

The Lord still stretches out his hand and touches people today. As we go through life and face problems big and small, we must learn to look to him. Then, not physically or visibly but through the ministry of the Holy Spirit, Jesus brings about those little stirrings and visitations we need. Hasn't that ever been your experience?

So many times I've been at the end of my resources, my circumstances overwhelming me. But as I've been studying the Word of God or praying or worshiping, suddenly the Lord, by his Spirit, has touched me and strengthened me for the road ahead. Immediately depression or turmoil has given way to joy. Out of nowhere, the touch of Jesus has changed my situation.

I've wondered, "What was that? What happened just then?" To use the words of a song that Bill Gaither wrote, all I can say is, "He touched me."[1] It's not emotionalism or fanaticism. It's a spiritual reality. "He touched me" is not only the testimony of the apostle John or a leper or blind person in the Bible—it can also be your testimony today.

Jesus, touch me. Touch my family. Lift me, heal me, and strengthen me with your joy and peace. I need your touch today.

5

REMEMBERED BY GOD

He remembered Abraham, and he brought Lot out.

GENESIS 19:29, NIV

All of us probably have family members—mothers and fathers, sons and daughters, brothers and sisters—who have never experienced God's salvation. They face an eternal destiny away from God, in a place where Jesus warned that there is nothing but punishment and suffering (see Matthew 25:30).

Abraham knew the pain of a relative being in a dangerous place. His nephew Lot had been traveling with him, but their cattle had become too numerous for the available water sources. So Abraham told Lot, "Look, let's go separate ways. You choose where you want to go, and I'll go the other direction." Lot saw that the plain of the Jordan was fertile land, and he chose it. Unfortunately, that's where the cities of Sodom and Gomorrah were located. The people there were sinning greatly against the Lord.

One day Abraham, who was called a friend of God, was visited by three angelic beings. One of them was the Lord himself. As the visitors were leaving, the Lord told Abraham, "I have heard a great outcry from Sodom and Gomorrah, because their sin is so flagrant. I am going down to see if their actions are as wicked as I have heard" (Genesis 18:20-21). Abraham realized, *Oh no. My nephew is in harm's way.*

That's when he began a unique set of prayers: "But wait, Lord," Abraham said. "God is just. Will you destroy the city if there are fifty righteous people there?"

The Lord answered, "If I find fifty righteous people in Sodom, I will spare the entire city for their sake" (Genesis 18:26).

Then Abraham asked the Lord if he would spare the city for forty-five righteous people. He continued asking, all the way down to ten people. The Lord answered, "I will not destroy it for the sake of the ten" (Genesis 18:32). Then he left.

The two angels went on to Sodom, where they were horribly threatened with a homosexual assault. The angels had to practically pull Lot and his family out of that depraved city, because even Lot was slow to respond to the sin around him. Needless to say, there were not ten righteous people there, and Sodom and Gomorrah were destroyed with burning sulfur from heaven.

But notice what Scripture says: "When God destroyed the cities of the plain, *he remembered Abraham*, and he brought Lot out of the catastrophe" (Genesis 19:29, NIV). Shouldn't it read, "He remembered Lot"? No, no, no. God remembered *Abraham*, and he delivered Lot. Abraham's prayer, his intercession, was the only reason Lot was delivered. God remembered Abraham pleading, interceding.

What does that say to us today? Jesus promised that judgment will one day come upon the people of this earth. Should we not take time today to intercede for those we love with persistence and faith? Then what the Bible says about Abraham and Lot can be said about us and our own family members: "God remembered *our* prayer and delivered ____________ out of the judgment they were heading to."

Oh, Lord, bring my family members to you.
Show them their need of a Savior. Only you
can open their hearts to the love of Christ.
Thank you, Jesus, that no matter how far from
you they are, you are able to save each one.

6

IMMOVABLE

The godly have deep roots.

PROVERBS 12:3

Our society these days is so up and down. People live in turmoil and anxiety. Even among believers in Christ, too many suffer from a lack of stability. They're fine one month, and the next month they're hardly living a victorious life of faith in Christ.

God wants us to be stable, fixed, immovable. But how do we hold steady in a world where everything is going crazy—the economy, politics, wars and rumors of wars? Proverbs 12:3 has the answer: "The godly have deep roots."

For plants, stability doesn't come from how pretty the leaves are or how red the apple looks. It's the root system that makes a tree secure. Some trees are quickly uprooted in a hurricane, while others stand firm. They bend, but they don't break because their roots go down deep.

It's the same in our Christian lives. Everything depends on our roots. So what is it about roots that we need to know?

First, roots are unseen. No one looks at a tree and says, "What beautiful roots!" Likewise, nobody sees a Christian's hidden life with the Lord. Two people at church could be worshiping God, and one is as unstable as can be while the other is like a tree planted by rivers of living water that won't be moved. What makes the difference? Their root structures—their private lives in the Word and in communion with the Lord.

Second, roots search for water. When we have our secret times with the Lord, we must not be rushed or mechanical. Rather, we need to drink again from the water of life and experience afresh the Spirit of God. The apostle Paul told us, "We were all given the one Spirit to drink" (1 Corinthians 12:13, NIV). We need unhurried, meaningful times alone with the Lord so we can get the watering, the fresh grace from God's Spirit, that we need for each day.

Third, when storms come, the roots of some trees go even deeper. It can be the same way with us. If we are believers with deep roots, storms don't knock us over. Instead, they strengthen us. When the winds beat against us, we can experience spiritual endurance as our roots sink further into the love and faithfulness of Christ.

What happens when we have shallow roots? Believers with shallow roots are spiritually unstable. One month they're on fire for God. The next, they're off the radar. They often get caught up with the winds of strange doctrines and get blown all around. Or an adverse situation arises, a bad memory resurfaces, an attack of Satan comes, and they lose their tempers or fall into a funk. What's wrong? Their roots need to go deeper.

Leonard Ravenhill, a well-known revival teacher and author, told me, "You know, Jim, the apostle Paul never said, 'Nothing hurts me.' He said, 'Nothing *moves* me.'" Yes, sometimes we cry. We feel righteous indignation. But we shouldn't let things move us. We've got to stay steadfast, letting our roots go deep down into the love and grace of Christ.

Lord, show me how to spend meaningful time with you each day so that my roots can go down deeper. I don't want to be tossed by the storms of life. Make me stronger and stronger so I can weather the storms of life.

7

PRAY FOR ME

Brothers and sisters, pray for us.

1 THESSALONIANS 5:25

The apostle Paul had a supernatural encounter with Christ on the road to Damascus. He became a leader in the church in Antioch, then went on several missionary trips and planted many churches. Later, he was even caught up to heaven and heard things he wasn't allowed to share with others. Eventually he wrote a good portion of the New Testament.

Yet with all his credentials, Paul said something that might be surprising to our ears: "Brothers and sisters, pray for us" (1 Thessalonians 5:25). He appealed to the believers he had led to Christ, urging them, "Join in my struggle by praying to God for me" (Romans 15:30).

"I mean, really, Paul," they could have said. "You're our spiritual father and a famous apostle. You need *us* to pray for *you*?"

Asking others to pray for us has almost become obsolete. What a terrible loss for us! God has given us the beautiful privilege of being helped by the prayers of fellow brothers and sisters. So why don't we ask for it?

For some of us, like me, it's probably spiritual pride. "No, I'm the pastor. I have this thing together." Or maybe we don't trust the power of prayer. We think, *I can handle this on my own.*

Years ago, I was scheduled to preach at Bill Gaither's Praise Gathering. I had prepared a word of encouragement to fit the praise and worship atmosphere there. But when I looked at my notes in my hotel room the night before, it's as if they were lifeless to me. I felt no inspiration at all.

So I began to pray. "God, I don't have notes for anything else. And this sermon seems to fit."

But the Lord laid on my heart something different. "No, I want you to preach that my house shall be called a house of prayer. Not a place to make money, not a place of entertainment, but a place for prayer." This would be a rather unusual topic in a room full of people who were there for multiple concerts over two or three days.

I paced and prayed for hours, my heart pounding. Around midnight, I said, "Oh, God, how can I preach that?" I imagined the audience walking out as I spoke. Suddenly a dark presence came into that room. I was in a battle. I walked; I wept; I called on God; I rebuked the devil.

Finally, at about three thirty in the morning, I got peace and fell asleep.

The phone rang at six. It was my wife, Carol, at home in New York. "What's going on?" she said. "I couldn't sleep all night. I've been praying for you. What's happening there?" She prayed a powerful prayer over me.

Later the video "My House Shall Be Called a House of Prayer"[2] went out in record-breaking numbers. Pastors called me for months, saying, "I showed the video of your message in our church, and prayer broke out in the service. People arriving for the next service had to wait because I couldn't get the first group out." To the glory of God, all this came about because in the midst of a strong spiritual battle, someone was praying for me.

Why don't we ask other Christians to pray for us more often than we've been doing? Paul knew that it was vitally important. So should we.

Lord, I don't ask others to pray for me as often as I should. Help me to humble myself. Show me what you will do when I have others interceding for me.

8

READY TO WORK

The harvest is great, but the workers are few.

MATTHEW 9:37

When Jesus looked at the crowds following him, he perceived that they were spiritually "harassed and helpless" (Matthew 9:36, NIV). Literally, this description could be rendered "mangled, exhausted, and thrown down." Then Jesus, moved with compassion, declared to his disciples, "Look, the harvest is great. But the workers are few."

People today, as in Jesus' day, are hurting and needing the love and hope Christ offers. The harvest is great, but as the Lord said two thousand years ago, the workers are few.

It seems like an oxymoron that God would need anything. But Jesus didn't tell his disciples to sit back and watch God save people all by himself. No, he said, "The workers are few," as if to say, "The work can't get done unless there are workers."

What do workers do? They work. So even though God has all power, and even though salvation is received as a gift, in order to get the gospel out, God needs people. He needs workers to share the good news, pray over others, follow up, keep at it, and spend time and energy toward the building up of God's Kingdom.

Over an Easter weekend at our church, more than a thousand people came forward to receive Christ after seeing our dramatic production, *The Story of Love*. Praise God! But what my daughter Sue and the team at our church did to put on the program—all the preparation, all the invitations, all the prayer—took a lot of labor. To do the work of ministry means to work. And according to Jesus, the workers are few.

The Lord wants us to refocus on what Christianity is all about. It's not "Give me, give me, give me." It's "Give me what I need so that I can work and bring glory to God as souls are saved." Luke 15:10 declares that the angels rejoice more when one soul repents than when we enjoy great Bible studies or worship services. Jesus came to seek and save the lost (see Luke 19:10).

Why don't we work for the Lord more than we do? Maybe we don't see the need as we should. Or maybe we're too lazy to expend energy for the cause of Christ. But what joy and fulfillment we miss by not laboring in the fields! As Psalm 126:6 says, "They sing as they return with the harvest."

The great Methodist circuit-riding preacher Francis Asbury declared to a gathering of young ministers who were going to serve like him, riding horses through rivers and other rough territory, "Although the devil attacks you in a thousand ways and there's discouragement on all sides, you'll never be happier than when you're doing the work of the Lord."

That's true for all of us. We're probably suffering a bit from a "Give me," "Fill me," "I have this problem," "I need a better job" attitude and have too little thought of the fields that are ripe unto harvest. We need to see people and feel for them, just as Christ does.

Jesus said, "We must quickly carry out the tasks assigned us by the one who sent us. The night is coming, and then no one can work" (John 9:4). Let's give ourselves to God and say, "Lord, here I am. I'm ready to do your work." We can't do it ourselves. But God will help every sincere worker in his fields.

Jesus, after the work you did for me on the cross, how can I not devote my life to extending your kingdom? Send more workers into your harvest field, Lord—and make me one of them.

9

LEARNING TO WAIT

The LORD said to my Lord, "Sit in the place of honor at my right hand until I humble your enemies."

ACTS 2:34-35

When I was a young pastor, an older minister told me, "You know, Jim, the hardest part of faith is waiting—and the hardest part of waiting is the last half hour."

Abraham, although God had promised him a son, had to wait for that baby. Joseph got two dreams from the Lord, but boy, did he have to wait (including in prison) before he saw his brothers bow down before him. Noah was told to build an ark because of a flood that would cover the earth, but he waited a hundred years before the rain started falling.

Even Jesus waits. In the first sermon of the Christian era, Peter quoted Psalm 110:1, indicating that Jesus had ascended to heaven and was now sitting at the Father's right hand, *waiting* for God to humble his enemies.

A lot of us want to walk by faith and not by sight. But when what we're trusting God for doesn't come to pass right away, we all too quickly give up. We need to learn to wait.

I used to go to the supermarket at eleven thirty at night just so I wouldn't have to wait in long lines. One night I loaded up my cart and headed for the only open register. But as I approached the checkout lane, a lady who was buying one of everything in the store appeared out of nowhere and slid in front of me. There I was, waiting at close to midnight!

We all tend to be impatient. But we can't be impatient with God. We need to trust the Lord and *keep* trusting him, even when the answer is long in coming.

Back in the seventies when our church was meeting in a YWCA auditorium, we discovered a big theater for sale on Flatbush Avenue. My father-in-law told me, "Look, that would be a great place for a church." I began to negotiate with the owner of the building, and we agreed on a price of $210,000. (That was a lot of money back then.)

While we were still figuring out details, the theater chain that was in the building called me. "Hey, Reverend, we hear you want to buy the theater. We've got three years left on our lease. How about a hundred thousand per year?"

I said, "What are you talking about?"

"Yeah, you didn't know we have a lease?"

I was crushed. The deal was off for us.

A year later, my father-in-law again saw a "For Sale" sign in front of the building. The theater chain had been mismanaging the place. I called the owner. He said, "Yeah, Reverend, let's talk. We agreed on $210,000, right?"

I said, "No. You've let the place get totally destroyed. I'll give you $150,000 cash."

"Reverend, come on. Let's split it. How about $180,000?"

I'm not a hard bargainer, but I had a sense that I should hold out. "Sir," I said, "if it's a dime more than $150,000, you can keep it."

"Reverend, you're a tough negotiator," he said. "Okay. You've got a deal."

So God saved us $60,000 because he forced us to wait.

God is so good. When we wait, he has something better for us than we ever could have hoped for.

Jesus, help me to wait for you and not be disheartened when I don't see answers to your promises right away. Thank you, Lord, that when I wait on you, I will never be disappointed.

10

KNOWING YOUR FUTURE

Surely your goodness and unfailing love will pursue me all the days of my life.

PSALM 23:6

All kinds of people today are consulting fortune tellers and psychics to give them a word about their future. Even among churchgoers, people are running around asking, "Where am I going to be five years from now?" Or they check their daily horoscopes, which is a terrible thing to do. "I'm a Taurus," people say. "I'm a Leo." No, you're a Christian. That's far better than any of the signs of the zodiac.

It's obvious that many people are fascinated with the future. But because it's unknown, it's easy to get anxious about it. We want to know what's going to happen. But today let's read what God promises us, which David declared: "Surely your goodness and unfailing love will pursue me all the days of my life" (Psalm 23:6).

Not maybe. Not possibly. *Surely* goodness and mercy. That's our future every day we live as children of our heavenly Father.

"But, Jim," you might say, "what if circumstances aren't looking favorable? Worse, what if the bottom seems to be falling out?" Well, difficulties are a form of God's goodness and unfailing love. The Lord allows them for a reason. But in the middle of the pain, there's a God-glorifying conclusion on its way. God is not a man; he cannot lie. He promised us goodness and mercy all the days of our lives, and his promises are unshakable. He will deliver.

What father or mother would say, "I love my children, but I want to see their lives ruined. I want the roof to fall in on them, and I'm not going to help them when it does"? No! If we, being evil, know how to give good gifts to our children, the Father knows how to deliver goodness and mercy to us on a daily basis.

Notice, goodness and mercy won't come sometime or other. They're right behind us. Some of us need to stop being focused on the devil and demonic activity. Instead, we need to recognize spiritually that right this minute, goodness and mercy are all around us. They're chasing us. We can't shake them.

We need to believe the Lord's guarantee of daily goodness and mercy. We should receive them and praise God for them even before they're fully manifested in our lives. Otherwise, we'll give in to anxious thoughts and worry.

When I counsel people who live with anxiety about the future and ask them what they're afraid of, some tell me, "I don't even know. I don't fear cancer or a natural disaster or war. But apprehension about the future just makes me lie awake at night, and my heart starts palpitating."

Here's your future: Surely goodness and mercy will follow you and your family, and me and my wife, Carol, and all God's people all the days of our lives, and we will dwell in the house of the Lord forever.

Lord, I worry sometimes about what will happen to me, my family, and our world. But you have promised that your goodness and mercy are right behind me, chasing me down. Thank you for giving me your peace as I leave the future in your loving hands.

11

WHEN YOU WANDER

Come and find me,
for I have not forgotten your commands.
PSALM 119:176

After writing the longest chapter in the Bible, including the verse, "I have hidden your word in my heart, that I might not sin against you" (Psalm 119:11), it's hard to believe that the psalmist ended with, "I have wandered away like a lost sheep; come and find me" (Psalm 119:176).

What a great encouragement for us. Even the man who had written all those wonderful verses came to a time in his life when he wrote, "I have wandered away like a lost sheep."

What did he wander away from, though? It was from the Lord and the walk of faith. Haven't we all done that at some point?

Notice, though, what the psalmist did: He acknowledged that he had wandered. How do we know that? Because the last phrase of the verse is "for I have not forgotten your commands." In other words, "I know your commands. I know your goodness, your holiness, your faithfulness. But oh, God, I have wandered."

Wandering doesn't happen overnight. It's like when a sheep sees a little green patch of grass and moves toward it. "Let me go over there. It's only a few feet away." Then he sees another tasty bit of turf. He starts to wander in that direction. Pretty soon, he's left the flock. Sheep do not exactly have high IQs. And sadly, we're like sheep. We wander from the Lord, and the next thing we know, we're heading toward major trouble with predators setting their sights on us.

But here's the beautiful part: The psalmist wrote, "Come and find me."

He didn't say, "Lord, I'm coming back!" No, he knew that when temptation, sin, or spiritual blindness causes us to wander, we can't always get back so easily, even if we still remember God's commands. Sometimes all we can say is, "Lord, come and find me. Put me on your shoulders and bring me home."

In college I was not a fervent Christian. I was caught up in playing basketball and trying to be a big man on campus. But oh, how empty I was inside. I was surrounded by secular people on a secular campus and prone to my own carnality and weakness. One night I lay in bed, feeling so miserable. I just had to say, "God, come and get me."

Some might argue, "You know what you're supposed to do! Just go and do it!" Yes, the prodigal son came to his senses and said, "I'm going to my father's house." But sometimes, even though we're willing to do right, we can't. We need the Lord's help. All we can do is say, "I've wandered, Lord, but I've not forgotten your commands. I'm humbling myself. Please come and get me. I'm in a trap. I can't get out that easily."

That's what the Israelites did when they had sinned. They cried to the Lord, "Turn me, and I will be turned" (Jeremiah 31:18, GW). In other words, "Lord, you've got to give us your mercy and grace."

If your heart is wandering today, catch yourself and confess it to the Lord. And if you're doing well, walking closely with the Lord, remember that if you wander one day, you can say, "Lord, I have wandered away like a lost sheep. Come and get me." He will.

Oh, Lord, I know your commands, but sometimes I still wander away from you. Thank you, Jesus, that when I get lost, you hear my cry, and in your mercy you come and get me. I love you, Lord.

12

STEPPING OUT IN FAITH

By faith . . . he went without knowing where he was going.

HEBREWS 11:8

We live in the day of GPS and Google Maps. But Abraham, who lived in the Old Testament times, used a different kind of guidance system: "It was by faith that Abraham obeyed when God called him to leave home and go to another land that God would give him as his inheritance. *He went without knowing where he was going"* (Hebrews 11:8).

Most folks are control freaks. We like to know not only where we're going but which route we'll take, where there's heavy traffic, and how long the trip will last. But if we're going to live by faith, then the experience of Abraham, the father of all who believe (see Romans 4:16), is a lesson for us.

Abraham was a pagan living in Ur of the Chaldees when God sovereignly approached him and said, "Leave."

"Leave what?"

"Leave everything—your house, your land, your culture, your food, your friends. Then go to a land that I will show you."

"Where is this land?"

"Don't worry about it. Just head west—I'll take care of the rest."

Imagine how his friends must have ridiculed him. Abraham got his caravan together, and he and his wife and nephew were about to head out, and someone said, "We're going to miss you, Abraham. By the way, where are you going?"

"Umm, I'm not sure. But I know who's going with me."

Maybe you sense that God wants you to step out in faith and do something he's called you to. You want to know how it will work out, but God is saying, "No, just take the next step by following me."

We can't prove God's leading by the scientific method. There's not a hope that we can convince someone empirically of the Lord's guidance in our lives. When God tells us to take a certain course, we need to rely on his love for us and trust that he knows best.

Carol and I felt called into the ministry even though I had no Bible school or seminary education and she had no formal music training. One very difficult day, I got up the courage to tell my mother, "Mom, I left my job. I'm going into the ministry. We're taking a church in downtown Brooklyn."

My mother knew that I had a college degree and had been working in the business world. She also knew that we had a baby. She said, "How are you going to live?"

It was hard to answer. I could hardly believe myself what we were doing. With emotion I told her, "We're going to live by faith."

In her Polish, practical way, my mother said, "And Jim, what does faith pay?" She meant that we had real bills and would need real money.

My mother later became our biggest supporter and also a member of the church. So many wonderful blessings followed, with many people converted. But when we started out, all we knew was that God was holding our hands.

When you know that something is God's will, step out. Don't let the unknown destination hold you back from obeying the Lord. He will bless your obedience as you follow him one step at a time.

God, help me not to question you when you direct my path. Let me be like Abraham, trusting you so fully that no uncertainty or fear will keep me from obeying you. Thank you, Jesus.

13

PRAYER FIRST

Devote yourselves to prayer.

COLOSSIANS 4:2

I love devotionals. One shelf in my office is filled with volumes of daily readings from people like F. B. Meyer, A. B. Simpson, and Frances Ridley Havergal. Every morning I take one, sit down in a chair, read the entry for the day, and meditate on it. Then I look up the Scripture for the entry and read that entire chapter from the Bible. This helps build my faith and helps me to pray better. I often sing along to gospel songs on YouTube as well. Then, by God's grace, I feel more prepared to face the day.

Every morning we get our bodies ready to face the day—we shower, we shave, we dress for our appointments. But it's much more important to prepare the inner person by spending time with God so that his Spirit can minister to our spirits and we can receive spiritual strength for the day. Then, whatever comes our way, we will be ready to meet the challenge.

Hudson Taylor, the famous nineteenth-century missionary to China, said, "Do not have your concert first, and then tune your instrument afterwards. Begin the day with the Word of God and prayer, and get first of all into harmony with Him."[3] When my wife, Carol, and I watched the London Symphony Orchestra play for an album of hers, no one asked the violinists, cellists, and horn players to tune their instruments at the end of the performance. No, they tuned their instruments *before* they played so that they would be ready to perform on pitch.

Is there one formula to it? No. Different people have done it in different ways. But I like what British evangelist George Müller said: "The first great and primary business to which I ought to attend every day [is] to have my soul happy in the Lord."[4] Personally, my worst days have been when I've been too busy to be with the Lord. And my best days have been when I've spent time with the Lord the night before or that morning. There's a poise in my spirit, a confidence in God, a happiness in my soul that keeps me from being ruffled, no matter what comes my way.

When we meet with God in the morning, big problems can come, but we are confident that God will take care of them. When we're not prepared, though, not walking in the Spirit, then a mosquito can buzz by, and we want to call 911. All day long we need "the love of God and the patient endurance that comes from Christ" (2 Thessalonians 3:5). But we only get those qualities from spending time with Jesus.

If we're going to devote ourselves to prayer, the main thing we need is discipline. The flesh doesn't want to spend time with God; it's always in a hurry. But as Paul told Timothy, "God has not given us a spirit of fear and timidity, but of power, love, and self-discipline" (2 Timothy 1:7). Let's pray today that God will help us to be with him more in prayer so that we'll be able to live Christ-honoring lives.

Lord, give me the discipline to spend time with you each day so that your joy, love, and patience will flow out of me, no matter what comes my way.

14

GRACE TO FIGHT

Hold on to what you have.

REVELATION 3:11

Joash was a child of seven when he began to reign over Judah. Because of his predecessors, the sacred Temple in Jerusalem was in a state of unholy disrepair. But Joash wouldn't leave it that way. Early in his reign, he told the priests, "Collect all the offerings brought to the LORD's Temple, and use some of it for repairs" (see 2 Kings 12:4-5).

For a while the priests used the money for their own needs. But Joash got after them. "Come on," he said, "let's get with it. You're not doing the work" (see 2 Kings 12:7). So the high priest took a chest and bored a hole in it. The people came and gave gladly, and laborers went to work restoring the Temple.

Much later though, out of nowhere, things took a downward turn. An enemy, King Hazael, attacked Jerusalem. And what did Joash do? He collected all the sacred objects that he and the former kings of Judah had dedicated for the Temple, and he sent them all to Hazael. "So Hazael called off his attack on Jerusalem" (2 Kings 12:18).

Joash had labored, persevered, and prioritized the rebuilding of God's Temple. But when he was attacked, instead of trusting the God who had helped him repair the Temple, he surrendered to fear and let go of all that was valuable in God's house!

Why would God put this story in the Bible?

An enemy stole from Joash—and Satan wants to steal from us today (see John 10:10). But the God who gives us grace to build up his Kingdom also wants to give us grace to stand our ground when we're under attack.

Jesus told the church in Philadelphia, "Hold on to what you have" (Revelation 3:11). Some versions say, "Hold fast" or "Hold tight." In other words, "Whatever you've attained in God, don't let the enemy take it." Unfortunately, Joash gave in to fear and went backwards. God wants us to persevere and not let the enemy rob us of the spiritual treasures we've received from him.

Remember, Satan isn't after our money, cars, or houses. His attack is spiritual and targets our relationship with Christ. Satan wants to extinguish our first love, our hunger for God's Word, our devotion to whatever ministry God has called us to, the spiritual lives of our family members.

Maybe we used to enjoy time in God's presence, but now we're barely in the Word or in prayer. Or we've raised our children, prayed over them, but now they're not serving the Lord. Yet instead of persevering in faith, we stop trusting the promises of God. "Well, that's it, I guess. It didn't work out like I wanted."

Our oldest daughter, Chrissy, was a model child. My wife and I dedicated her to the Lord and raised her in the ways of God. But then the enemy came in, and she got away from us and from God, and soon we were estranged from her. But we didn't give up. The same God who had helped us raise her gave us the grace, thankfully, to see her recovered. And God brought her back.

Why don't you draw a line in the sand today regarding some aspect of your life in which you need to persevere—your love for God, your service for him, the spiritual condition of your son or daughter or spouse? Let's hold on to what we have in the Lord.

Lord, rescue the stolen property in my life. I will hold fast to you, Jesus, in prayer and faith, and trust you to bring great glory to your name.

15

THE UPWARD GLANCE

I lift up my eyes to the mountains.

PSALM 121:1, NIV

All through high school and college I played basketball. One of the cardinal rules of ballhandling is to keep your eyes up and not on the ball you're dribbling. If you keep your head down, you can't see your teammates or the basket—or where best to move on the court.

Over and over, the Bible likens the physical to the spiritual and asks, "What are the eyes of your heart looking at?" Faced with difficulties, the psalmist wrote, "I look up to the mountains—does my help come from there? My help comes from the Lord, who made heaven and earth!" (Psalm 121:1-2). "I'm going to look up to God," he said, "and keep looking for his faithfulness in my life."

Our eyes can look at the news and read what's happening with the economy, in the Middle East, in the government. It can depress our hearts and take away our joy and peace—unless we lift up our eyes to the mountains. It's easier for us to look straight ahead at the facts or down at possible negative scenarios, but we need to remind ourselves, by the grace of God, to keep our eyes up, toward the Lord.

Notice that the psalmist took decisive action: "I lift up my eyes." When we face a tough situation, if we look forward or sideways, we can get dejected and start looking down. Instead, we can boldly declare, "God, you see this problem I'm facing. I lift my eyes to heaven, because my help comes from you."

Notice also that the psalmist had the humility to know he needed help. Sometimes we get into difficult spots, and we won't lift our eyes to the Lord because we think we can handle things on our own. We need to realize that our bank accounts can't solve our problems. Our friends can't fix them. We need to look up in faith to God.

It's important to note that the psalmist had no plan B. He didn't say, "My help comes from you, Lord, but in case you don't help me out, here's my contingency plan." In our time of need, we must look singularly to God for his help. The early Christian church had no financial help, no political allies. They kept looking in faith to the Lord, and in the book of Acts, we read what wonders God worked through them.

We tend to look to God more readily during emergencies. When my wife and I counted our first offering of eighty-five dollars in that depressing little Brooklyn church, don't you think we knew that our help had to come from the Lord? How were we going to lead a church, pay the bills, and raise a family on eighty-five-dollar offerings? The Lord permits problems in our lives because he loves for us to repeat with the psalmist, "My help comes from you, Lord."

Now our offerings are much more, but the Spirit keeps reminding me, "Don't trust in the offerings or in the fact that things are better. Keep lifting your eyes up. You need the Lord." Whether we're in a crisis or doing well, we need to look up, and keep looking up. Our help comes from God.

Lord, sometimes my need is small, and sometimes it's an emergency, but every day I need your help. God, I look up to you today. My help comes from you and no one else.

16

A SACRIFICE OF THANKS

Make thankfulness your sacrifice to God.

PSALM 50:14

We find an interesting picture of the Lord in Psalm 50. Almighty God, the judge of the whole world, appears in a courtroom scene, where he has summoned the entire earth. But instead of judging the ungodly first, as we might imagine, "he calls on the heavens above and earth below to witness the judgment of his people" (Psalm 50:4). Judgment has to begin in the house of the Lord.

What was God's charge against his people? He didn't accuse them of unfaithfulness to Israel's sacrificial system (see Psalm 50:8). No, the problem lay in another area. "Listen, I don't need the bulls and goats you offer," God said. "Every animal in the forest is mine! The sacrifice I want from you is a thankful heart" (see Psalm 50:9-14).

Israel was adhering perfectly to their God-given worship system, but they were merely going through the motions. The Lord told them, "You offer me animal sacrifices, but you aren't thankful in your hearts for all I've done for you."

What is a sacrifice of thanksgiving? It's taking time to thank God from our hearts for his blessings.

You might say, "But God knows I'm thankful in my heart."

But the Lord says, "No, you must express your thanksgiving in an act of gratitude."

When God's people placed an offering before him, it was an apparent act of worship. But what God really desires is for us to come into his presence daily with hearts of sincere thanks to our loving Father.

Think of this: How much time do we really spend thanking God for all he's done and the prayers he's answered? Too often we bounce from one problem to another and forget to thank the Lord for what he's already done. That's been a besetting sin in my life. It's like the ten lepers; Jesus healed them all, but only one came back to say thanks. The Lord said, "Wait a minute. Where are the other nine?" They were too busy celebrating to thank the Lord.

I once counseled someone who said, "Oh, Pastor, pray that I get a job. I've been without work for six months." God came through with a beautiful job, and do you think the person was in church giving God thanks and praise? Not a chance. No, he had moved on to some new problem: "You've got to meet my boss. I can't take his attitude." Wait a minute. The man had no job, and now he's complaining about his new job? Isn't it true that we're better at complaining than giving thanks to God?

Giving thanks is all-important to our spiritual lives. In fact, failing to give God thanks is what started people turning away from the Lord, according to the apostle Paul (see Romans 1:21). Israel knew that God existed, but they would not worship him or *give him thanks*!

It's like a child who isn't thankful to his parents. The mother nursed her baby and walked the floor with him when he was sick. The father taught him to ride a bike and was there for all his baseball games. Now the child is older and has no time to honor his parents. How horrible!

Let's give God thanks for everything, little or big. How about the last breath we took, the clothes we're wearing, the bed we slept on last night—and most of all, our salvation through Jesus Christ? Every day we should take time to thank God. He's the giver of every good gift.

Lord, your Word says, "In everything give thanks," but sometimes I spend more time complaining than thanking you. Give me a thankful spirit, starting today.

17

FILLED WITH JOY

The believers were filled with joy and with the Holy Spirit.

ACTS 13:52

One of the marks of a person who has experienced salvation through Jesus Christ is a new spiritual joy. This is because the Holy Spirit lives within him, and the Spirit produces fruit—which includes joy (see Galatians 5:22). Anyone who really knows God should be a joyful person.

This "joy of the LORD" is our strength (Nehemiah 8:10). So whenever we are not joyful in spirit, we are weakened spiritually. This makes us more susceptible to satanic assaults. Not only that, but sad, gloomy, and irritable believers make a poor advertisement for Jesus Christ.

Advertisers trying to sell cars film a shiny, sleek car on a highway, with the light hitting it perfectly. Why? They want that car to draw you in. "I've got to have that," they want you to say. "That's a good-looking car."

We are Christ's ambassadors. How well do we represent him? Are we short-tempered, irritable, or depressed? Or are we expressing the joy of the Lord?

During Paul's first missionary journey, the Jews in Pisidian Antioch incited a mob against the new believers and drove Paul and Barnabas out of town. The Christians could have become fearful, but instead they "were filled with joy and with the Holy Spirit" (Acts 13:52). This was how Paul described that early Christian church. They were facing persecution, without much money, opposed by everyone, threatened with the loss of their jobs. Yet the report of Paul's missionary trip was not about how many were coming to church or what kind of buildings the church had. It was that "the abundant presence of the Holy Spirit in their lives" (Acts 13:52, CEB) was causing the believers to overflow with joy.

Can that be said about us today? Let's ask the Lord to revive us spiritually so our joy overflows! Then we can represent Christ in a way that will make salvation in him attractive.

What a terrible representation some of us make of the one we belong to. Too many of us live with a victim mentality. But we're not victims. We're Christians. What did Paul and Silas do at midnight, in prison, after being beaten? They sang with joy!

That joy can be ours today, but we have to claim it: "I will not walk depressed. I will not be gloomy. Holy Spirit, come and so fill me that your joy will overflow from my life. That is my badge. That is my advertisement for Jesus Christ."

What happened to that joyful song you once had? You went about your day singing. When we cease singing joyfully, we are not a good advertisement for Jesus Christ. May God help us to catch ourselves and say, "Lord, turn this thing around now." Like David in Psalm 51:12, let's ask God, "Restore to me the joy of your salvation."

Lord, fill me again with your Holy Spirit so that your joy will overflow from my life. Help me shake off gloominess, anger, and depression and claim the joy that is mine in Christ. Let my life represent you so that people will be drawn to you.

18

GOD LOVES YOU

Nothing can ever separate us from God's love.

ROMANS 8:38

God is love. His love for us doesn't change. The love of God is so certain, the apostle Paul wrote, that "neither death nor life, neither angels nor demons, neither our fears for today nor our worries about tomorrow—not even the powers of hell can separate us from God's love" (Romans 8:38).

When we get saved, we learn from John 3:16 that God loved us so much that he gave his Son to die for us. And we read in 1 John 3:1, "See how very much our Father loves us, for he calls us his children, and that is what we are!" What comfort that brings. We depend on God's love and faithfulness, not on our own strength or resolve.

But what happens when we don't sense God's love—or when we question whether we're loved by him at all?

A lot of Christians live days, even weeks, wondering whether God loves them because they don't feel his love. They go by their feelings, not by what God has said about who he is. But part of being spiritually mature means realizing that losing the sense of God's love doesn't mean that his love has disappeared.

The sun is shining one day, and we have a great time at the beach. The next day, it's dark and gloomy. Only a child would say, "The sun isn't there anymore." Of course it is. It's just that the clouds are blocking our awareness of it.

We must not be like that with the Lord. Some days we're on the mountaintop, and we're filled with the sweet awareness that God dearly loves us. Other days physical maladies or emotional stresses weigh us down, and we lose our sense of the Lord's deep concern for us.

Sometimes we don't sense God's love because we've sinned and feel that God has turned his back on us. But even then, God's unfathomable love for us has not changed. And if we confess our sin, as David did, God will have mercy on us because of his "unfailing love" (Psalm 51:1).

We need to understand that the surest thing in this world is that God loves us. He wants us to learn to walk by faith in that love, not by feelings. God's love has nothing to do with our feelings.

At times I've gotten up to preach, and because of heartache or some pressure on me, I've had little sense of God's love for me or even God's presence to help me. I've been almost numb inside because of the strain. But I've preached, and God has blessed the teaching by drawing people to himself. God has reminded me, "You don't have to feel my love. Just count on my love."

Every day, every hour, every minute, we need to repeat, "God is with me, whether I feel him or not. Jesus said that he would never leave me or forsake me. All his thoughts of me are thoughts of love." After all, "No power in the sky above or in the earth below—indeed, nothing in all creation will ever be able to separate us from the love of God that is revealed in Christ Jesus our Lord" (Romans 8:39). Just because the clouds are there doesn't mean the sun isn't shining.

Lord, help me to learn that nothing can ever separate me from your love. Teach me that your love is absolutely certain, even when I don't feel it. Thank you that I can count on your love for me.

19

DOING GOD'S WILL

I am fed by doing the will of the one who sent me and by completing his work.

JOHN 4:34, CEB

When we exercise, travel, or have a hard day at work, the strain on our bodies must be counterbalanced by rest and food. Jesus' disciples understood this. That's why during a long, hot trip through Samaria, while Jesus rested by a well, they went into a village to get food.

While they were gone, Jesus began talking to a woman who had come to draw water. He told her about living water and said that if she drank it, she would never thirst again. The woman went back into town to tell people, "Come and see a man who told me everything I ever did! Could he possibly be the Messiah?" (John 4:29). So people came streaming to meet the man at the well.

Jesus was dead tired and thirsty. But when an opportunity came for him to minister, he took it.

The disciples came back and said, "Rabbi, we got you some food."

Jesus replied, "I have food that you don't even know about."

"Did someone else bring him food?" they asked each other.

But Jesus told them, "I am fed by doing the will of the one who sent me and by completing his work" (John 4:34, CEB).

How could a person get nourishment from expending spiritual energy?

The truth is, finding out God's will for our lives and then giving ourselves to it is how we're spiritually nourished and fulfilled. We don't get fed only by reading the Bible and devotional books or by being in church, but by actually doing the will of God for our lives. Yes, we need to renew our inner person through times alone with God, but there is a nourishment, a satisfaction, that comes from doing. Doing what? The will of God.

Later on, Jesus told his followers, "As the Father has sent me, so I am sending you" (John 20:21). Jesus was sent to do God's work—and now he has sent *us* to fulfill his plan. God has some work for each of us to fulfill. And if we shirk it, we won't save energy. We'll lose nourishment, because Jesus said, "My nourishment is to *do* the will of God."

Many Christians are weak and sluggish because, to begin with, they don't even know the will of God for their lives. Every one of us needs to know God's will for us and then give ourselves to it. As we do, we'll find fulfillment and a spiritual impartation of strength.

God has wonderfully done that for me. When our church was in its former building and large crowds were coming in, I ended up doing four services every Sunday, each two hours long. I was physically and emotionally fatigued—absolutely. But because that's what God had called me to do, when I finally lay down in bed on Sunday nights, I was fulfilled. Oh, how I was refreshed, even though I was extremely tired!

You are called. Find out what God wants you to do and give yourself to it. Yes, you'll face attacks. People might oppose you, like they did our Lord. But there's nothing sweeter than *doing* the will of God.

God, I don't want to sit back and grow weak spiritually. Show me your will for my life and help me do it. I want the nourishment that comes from doing what you have called me to do.

20

DIVINE DISCIPLINE

God's discipline is always good for us.

HEBREWS 12:10

One of the outstanding dramatic moments in Old Testament history happened when Israel stubbornly refused to listen to God. They rejected his covenant with them, despised his warnings through the prophets, and worshiped worthless idols—and it led to disaster.

After Solomon's death, Israel was divided into two kingdoms. The northern kingdom was called Israel, and the southern one was called Judah. The northern kingdom, from the beginning, turned away from the true worship of God as laid down by the Lord to Moses. Instead, they let themselves be led into mixing the worship of idols with the worship of Jehovah.

God, in his love, sent prophets to the northern kingdom, one after another, warning them, pleading with them, "Turn back to me." Those ten tribes were still his covenant people, and he loved them. God warned them, "If you mix your worship of me with idol worship and then turn away from me, it will surely end in disaster."

But God's warnings were to no avail. So, sure enough, the Assyrian Empire laid siege to Samaria. Eventually the city fell, and its people were taken captive. The Assyrian king then dispersed the people of Israel all over the vast Assyrian Empire. The northern kingdom, which had existed for centuries, ceased to exist.

If we looked at this geopolitically, we would say that the Assyrian Empire was stronger than Israel. They conquered Israel with their military prowess. Through their strategy the northern kingdom became their subjects.

But the problem wasn't horizontal. It was vertical.

Some things that happen on earth have their seed, or genesis, when people lose the favor of God. Israel went into captivity not because Assyria was so powerful but because they turned from the Lord, and as a result, God removed his hand of blessing and protection from them. Although they were God's covenant people, the judgment could not be escaped.

This is clearly seen in 2 Kings 17:12: "Yes, they worshiped idols, despite the Lord's specific and repeated warnings." Interestingly, that Hebrew term for *idols* can be translated "round things," which can allude to dung. Israel turned away from the true worship of the invisible Almighty God, who loved them, and they ended up worshiping what amounted to mounds of dung! When we turn away from God, the ending is always tragic.

Not only did they turn away from God, but "they despised all his warnings" (2 Kings 17:15) and imitated the examples of the nations around them.

How can this encourage us today?

God loves us so much that when he sees us going the wrong way, he sends us warnings—flashing lights—saying, "This is wrong! Turn back. Repent." He's not trying to rain on our parade but to save us from certain judgment. We ought to be sensitive to God's whispers and warnings. They are signs that the Lord loves us. His love is a strong, persistent love.

Because that is true, we should treasure the conviction of God. When he sends us messengers—through a sermon, a book, a song, a troubled conscience, a whisper from the Spirit—let's not be stubborn and turn our backs on him. Instead, let's say, "God, thank you for your love. I'm coming back to the one who loves me the most."

Lord, give me a tender heart. I want you to correct me, even when it hurts. Help me to remember that your discipline is a sign of your love for me.

21

ALL IN ONE VERSE

Do to others whatever you would like them to do to you.

MATTHEW 7:12

There's a great way to summarize the entire Old Testament and its 613 commands in one sentence. Impossible, you say? No, everything in the law of Moses and the prophets is expressed in one verse.

Jesus made this simple statement in Matthew 7:12: "Do to others whatever you would like them to do to you." The verse goes on to say, "This is the essence of all that is taught in the law and the prophets." In other words, this statement sums up everything in the Old Testament about how God wants us to live.

True Christianity always results in new behavior patterns. Essentially, it's not about a doctrinal position. It's measured by how we treat the other people in our lives.

In fact, how we deal with other people reflects how much we really love God. Any other approach to the Christian life is a spiritual deception. "Oh, I love God. I love to study his Word and be in his presence. I just can't stand Barbara over there." And then we gossip about Barbara and destroy her reputation, all the time deceiving ourselves about our devotion to Christ.

God loves people, and when we treat them well, it brings him great joy. Do you want to make God happy? You don't have to read all the minor and major prophets in one sitting. You don't have to follow every command of Old Testament law. You just need to understand the essence of them all: "Do to others whatever you would like them to do to you."

It's all about treating others as we would want to be treated. Do we like people to talk about us behind our backs? No? Then let's not do that to them. Do we like people to encourage and compliment us? Then let's speak well of them.

"I know," someone will say, "but you don't know my brother-in-law."

No, I don't. But the Bible doesn't say who. It's just "Do to others"—all others—"whatever you would like them to do to you."

We live in a narcissistic culture. People are so wrapped up in themselves that they tend not to think about others and their problems. But we Christians should say, "Wait a minute. How would I want that person to treat me if I were down in the dumps? I would want them to lift me up."

Many are preoccupied with five-point Calvinism or the meaning of the mark of the beast in Revelation. Well, those things have their place. But the main thing is the main thing. Jesus summarized it in the simple command to treat others as we want to be treated.

Of course, this is easier said than done, especially with people who are nasty or have hard feelings toward us. Most of us have an inner circle of friends, where it's all about "You love me; I love you." But God sends sunshine on both the evil and the good. We've got to see beyond our little circles, because the Bible makes it universal—we should treat *all* others the same way we would like them to treat us.

Loving people, including those who aren't kind to us, is a sign of spiritual maturity. And it sums up 613 commands.

God, I want to make you happy. Fill me with your love for others. Help me to treat every person, whether it's easy or hard, the way I want to be treated.

22

A SENSE OF NEED

O God, be merciful to me, for I am a sinner.

LUKE 18:13

Jesus told a parable about prayer, and in it he gave an odd comparison. Two men, he said, went to the Temple to pray. One was a Pharisee—an extremely orthodox Jewish leader. The other was a despised tax collector.

The Jews in Jesus' day were in awe of the Pharisees. Unfortunately, this man's prayer was a performance, because all he did was recite his religious credentials: "I thank you, God, that I am not like other people—cheaters, sinners, adulterers. I'm certainly not like that tax collector! I fast twice a week, and I give you a tenth of my income" (Luke 18:11-12).

Unlike Pharisees, Jewish tax collectors were hated by everybody because they often cheated their own people. The Romans employed them to raise money for the empire, so the Jews resented them because they represented the oppressive ruling power. Yet with deep sincerity, this tax collector in the Temple humbly beat his breast and simply said, "O God, be merciful to me, for I am a sinner" (Luke 18:13).

Self-righteous people like the Pharisee in this story can't really pray authentically. They're so sure of their moral superiority that they have no sense of their need for God's mercy. The essence of prayer is expressing the need of our hearts. The Pharisee had no awareness of his spiritual condition because he thought he was better than everyone else.

The culture around us defines success as never feeling need. If you're a multimillionaire, have a superyacht, or own a fleet of luxury cars, people think you've made it. But spiritually, success is the exact opposite. Jesus' first words in the Sermon on the Mount are "Blessed are the poor in spirit" (Matthew 5:3, NIV). Literally, Jesus was saying, "Blessed are the beggars," or, as the Amplified Bible calls them, "the humble, who rate themselves insignificant."

How can the needy be the blessed ones? Because a sense of our need for God's help enables us to do the highest and most blessed thing a person can do on earth—which is to *pray*.

We must always remember that God resists the proud. The Pharisee in Jesus' parable recited his accomplishments, and he went home with nothing except God's displeasure. But God gives grace to the humble (see James 4:6). That's why Jesus said, "I tell you, this sinner, not the Pharisee, returned home justified before God" (Luke 18:14).

God has kept my wife and me ministering for a lot of years in downtown Brooklyn. But in the early days, our situation was depressing. No one had to tell us, "You really need God." Our problems drove us to him. Affluence, on the other hand, can be a detriment, because it takes away that precious sense of "I need thee, oh, I need thee; every hour I need thee."[5]

You and I can make today a day of communion and prayer with the Most High God. We can receive things beyond our imagination if we will just remember that when we humble ourselves and draw near to God, he will most certainly draw near to us.

Oh, Lord, give me the humility that senses its need of your help. Thank you for being a God who desires to bless those who come with nothing in their hands.

23

A GIFT FROM THE FATHER

How much more will your heavenly Father give the Holy Spirit to those who ask him.

LUKE 11:13

What is the best gift God could give us? Jesus showed us when he taught his disciples to pray: "If you sinful people know how to give good gifts to your children, how much more will your heavenly Father give the Holy Spirit to those who ask him" (Luke 11:13). The choicest gift God could give us is more of the Holy Spirit.

Most believers today, though, don't start the day by praying, "Lord, fill me with the Holy Spirit." Even though the Spirit is a gift—we don't earn his presence and power in our lives—Jesus told us, "Ask for him." If we ask, we'll receive from our Father the Holy Spirit in measure according to our faith and need.

Just before Jesus went back to heaven, he told his disciples, "The Father will give you another helper, the Holy Spirit, in my place" (see John 14:16, GW). So in reality, how we relate to the Holy Spirit is exactly how we treat Jesus Christ. We can't say we love Jesus if we reject the helper he sent. No, the Holy Spirit is the Spirit of Christ (see Romans 8:9). Just as the disciples cherished the Lord here on earth, so we are to cherish the presence of the Holy Spirit.

The Spirit was sent by Christ to accomplish several things in our lives.

When we are full of the Holy Spirit, he makes us aware of the shortness of time before Christ's return. We live more for the moment, because we understand that today is the only day we have. Yesterday is over, and tomorrow is not promised. We realize that eternity is at the door, as the apostle Paul wrote in Philippians 4:5: "Remember, the Lord is coming soon." Realizing this truth changes how we spend our time and money. No preacher or sermon in itself can make the shortness of time real to our hearts. This spiritual reality comes only through the Holy Spirit's ministry.

The Spirit also makes us aware that Jesus is with us. The Lord said, "Never will I leave you; never will I forsake you" (Hebrews 13:5, NIV). Yes, Jesus is in heaven, but he's also with us through the presence of the Holy Spirit. His nearness comforts and strengthens us, as it did David, who wrote, "I know the LORD is always with me. I will not be shaken, for he is right beside me" (Psalm 16:8). Knowing that Jesus is always by our side alters our words, deeds, plans, priorities, and reactions.

The Holy Spirit gives us an ear to hear what he is saying to the churches—and to us individually. It's mentioned seven times in Revelation: "Anyone with ears to hear must listen to the Spirit and understand what he is saying to the churches" (Revelation 2:7, 11, 17, 29; 3:6, 13, 22). Jesus was speaking here about the ears of a person's inner spirit. When our hearts are quickened by the Holy Spirit, we can comprehend what God is saying in our own lives and times.

The greatest need of every church isn't money or people. Our greatest need is for a visitation of the Spirit. A new experience of the power of the Holy Spirit changes everything, because it lifts us above the merely physical world and enables us to live and walk with God in the Spirit.

Lord, fill me with the Holy Spirit today.
I can do nothing without him.

24

LAST WORDS

You will be my witnesses, telling people about me everywhere.

ACTS 1:8

When a person is about to die, he doesn't call his family around and say, "Please take out the trash when I'm gone." He talks about what's most important to him. In a similar way, the last recorded words of Jesus Christ before he left the earth carry great weight.

As Jesus was about to return to heaven, the disciples asked him, "When will the Roman Empire be thrown off our necks and Israel go back to the good old days of being a sovereign nation with a king?" (see Acts 1:6). They wanted it right then, because they thought that was the role of the Messiah.

But Jesus declared an important truth: "The Father *alone* has the authority to set those dates and times, and they are not for you to know." Then he told them what they *needed* to know: "You will receive power when the Holy Spirit comes upon you. *And you will be my witnesses, telling people about me everywhere"* (Acts 1:7-8).

Our goal today is not to figure out all the mysterious symbols in the book of Revelation or who the Antichrist is going to be. In fact, over the last 120 years of Christian history, whenever gifted teachers have tried to fit verses into their own historical contexts or make authoritative predictions, it has ended up embarrassing both them and the church of Christ. "Wait," people say, "I thought you said that Mussolini [or Hitler, Stalin, etc.] was the Antichrist! Why were you so sure and yet so wrong?"

We should also remember that the event that makes the angels rejoice is not a good Bible study or even a good prayer meeting—it's when we tell one person about Jesus and that person repents and puts his or her faith in the Lord. We must be careful not to be distracted from what Jesus directed his followers to do.

Notice what else Jesus said: The disciples were to tell others about him "everywhere—in Jerusalem, throughout Judea, in Samaria, and to the ends of the earth" (Acts 1:8). The command he gave was to spread the gospel to all people, even in the remotest parts of the earth. Now it's very unlikely that any of us will be called by God to Siberia or South Africa. But how about first being faithful to tell people about Jesus "in Jerusalem"—in other words, right where we live today.

We all can do that. Not everyone is called to be a full-time missionary or pastor or evangelist. But each one of us can tell people we encounter about Jesus—who he is, how he lived, the miracles that confirmed who he was, the meaning of the cross and his blood, how he rose from the dead, that he's coming back again—and what he's done in our lives. We can start doing that today in our own Jerusalem as he helps us.

Let's not get distraught over world events or be taken up with the guessing game of prophetic calendars. Instead, let's remember *the last words Jesus said*: "In Jerusalem, Judea, Samaria, and to the ends of the earth, tell people about Jesus." The Christian church is shrinking in America, and converts are not being made as they could be if we were to keep first things first. Let's tell people about Jesus.

God, help me to tell someone about Jesus today.
Help me to take your final words on earth to
heart and to be your witness right where I am.

25

TRANSFORMED BY GOD

We all . . . are being transformed into his image with ever-increasing glory.

2 CORINTHIANS 3:18, NIV

Have you ever gotten discouraged by your lack of progress in the Christian life? Maybe you've then said, "That's it. I'm turning over a new leaf. Come on, I'm going to read more of the Bible, starting today! I haven't been serious about spiritual things, but that's about to change. No more angry outbursts. Bad habits are stopping right now." When we do this, we mean well. But making vows to change our behavior patterns is not God's way of making us more like Christ.

Under the old covenant, or Old Testament law, people promised and tried hard to obey the commands of God. Yet while the law reflected the holiness of God, there was an underlying problem. The law provided no spiritual strength to help them obey God's commands.

But praise God, the Lord promised in the Old Testament that one day he would make a new covenant with his people—a covenant much different from and far superior to the first one. And the most glorious point of the new covenant, what makes it so wonderful, is that God himself transforms born-again Christians into the image of Christ by his Holy Spirit and not by our self-effort.

Rightly dividing the Word of God has a lot to do with understanding the difference between the old and new covenants. The old covenant showed people their sin but gave them no power to overcome it. But when Paul wrote about "the overwhelming glory of the new way" (2 Corinthians 3:10), he showed us how different that way is: "We all, who with unveiled faces contemplate the Lord's glory, are being transformed into his image with ever-increasing glory" (2 Corinthians 3:18, NIV).

But notice this: The Greek term for "being transformed" is in the passive form. That means that the action is being done *to* us, not *by* us. In other words, we don't transform ourselves. No, the transforming is done to us *by God.*

Growth in the spiritual life is not about vows and promises. It's about letting God, through the Holy Spirit, transform our lives. We'll never change ourselves by self-effort, making promises, or gritting our teeth. It has to be done *to* us by God's wonderful grace—the same grace that brought us into his family.

Over the years I have counseled so many people who sincerely love the Lord and want to be different. Unfortunately, they try to accomplish the change through their own efforts. When they came to Jesus as helpless sinners, they knew they couldn't pay the price for their sins—only God could. The action was done *to* them. But once they started walking with the Lord and desiring to be more like Christ—which was a sign that God was working *in* them—they slipped back to the old way of more effort, more trying, more telling God, "I promise I'll live better today!" How often we forget what Jesus said: "Apart from me you can do nothing" (John 15:5).

Romans 12:2 sums it up: "Don't copy the behavior and customs of this world, but let God transform you into a new person by changing the way you think." Let's allow God to transform us today. Let's keep trusting him to do his work.

Lord, thank you for the new covenant that provides pardon for my sin and transforms me into the image of Christ. Help me not to trust in my strength, but to let you change me today.

26

THE BEST WAY OF LIFE

Love . . . is not irritable.

1 CORINTHIANS 13:4-5

The Corinthian church was very much taken up with *charismata*—the gifts of the Holy Spirit given to the church after Christ ascended back to heaven. But unfortunately they were abusing the gifts of the Spirit and bringing confusion into their services. So Paul, in 1 Corinthians 12, wrote to clarify all the powerful things the Holy Spirit wants to do in gifting believers and calling us to various kinds of ministries. Then in 1 Corinthians 14 he addressed the abuses and how to correct them. Between these two chapters, however, seemingly out of nowhere, Paul stated, "But now let me show you a way of life that is best of all" (1 Corinthians 12:31).

Paul began chapter 13 with a warning: A person can understand all mysteries, speak in the tongues of men and angels, have faith to move mountains, or even prophesy—but if he lacks love, it's all for naught. He's a zero. A clanging cymbal. Most of us in church admire the person who speaks with polished phrases, or someone who has the gift of faith, or a person God uses to heal others. But while Paul encouraged the believers in Corinth to pursue Holy Spirit gifting (see 1 Corinthians 14:1), he stated emphatically that love is the best way of all.

This shows us that every person in the body of Christ can aspire to greatness before God. Greatness in God's eyes is not having a particular spiritual gift, or being a pastor, or writing a book. It's practicing love, which is God's very essence. God is not a prophecy. God is not a miracle. God is love—*agape* love.

Then Paul described what this kind of love looks like so the church could know how to identify it. One of the signs of a loving Christian is that he or she is "not irritable" (1 Corinthians 13:5). The NIV has "not easily angered," and Phillips has "not touchy."

We've all known people who have made us feel like we had to walk on eggshells around them. Any little sentence sets them off. They remind me of a Spanish word I learned in Argentina—*fosforito*. It means "matchstick." When someone says, "Watch it, he's a fosforito," they mean that if you rub that person the wrong way, the friction will produce red-hot flames. Love is the opposite of that.

Jesus was never irritable or touchy. Being that way is actually a form of pride. It imposes on the people around us, "You will put up with my mood and my irritability. I don't care what you're going through, because something has rubbed me the wrong way, and I will vent my displeasure." That's very carnal—yet, according to 1 Corinthians 13, it can exist along with great faith and understanding Bible mysteries.

The sign of maturity is not Bible knowledge. Paul made that clear in 1 Corinthians 8:1: "While knowledge makes us feel important, it is love that strengthens the church." And God's kind of love is not touchy.

Oh, Lord, I do want to pursue the gifts of the Spirit, as you commanded, but more than that, I want to love like you do. Help me not to be irritable with others. Instead, fill me with your love.

27

PRAYER FROM DEEP INSIDE

Hannah was praying in her heart.

1 SAMUEL 1:13, NIV

Hannah badly wanted a child, but she couldn't have one. Every year she went with her husband, Elkanah, and his other wife, Peninnah, to the Tabernacle at Shiloh. The Tabernacle was the Old Testament place of worship before the Temple was built in Jerusalem. But year after year, Peninnah mocked Hannah for being barren.

So one day, while the family was eating at the Tabernacle, Hannah got up and went to pray. She prayed in her heart—her lips moved, but there was no sound.

The high priest, Eli, saw her and thought she was drunk. "Why do you come into the Tabernacle when you're drunk?" he said to her.

"No," Hannah said. "I've been pouring out my heart to God" (see 1 Samuel 1:1-16).

Hannah's prayer of faith came from deep inside, and God answered her. In doing so, God changed the history of the Old Testament. Hannah's son, Samuel, came on the scene during the dark days of the judges, and he brought about a turning back to God in Israel. Some call him the founder of the school of the prophets.

Samuel Rutherford, a Scottish pastor and theologian, said, "Words are but accidents of prayer."[6] Real prayer, the prayer that God honors, comes from our innermost hearts, and many times it can't find utterance in words. It comes with tears or sometimes with Holy Spirit–inspired groans too deep to be spoken (see Romans 8:26).

Rather than hearing us say surface prayers, God, through the Spirit, wants to lead us into time with him when the greatest longings of our hearts can be expressed in prayer.

I've had needs in my life, especially as a young pastor, that have caused me to pray with hot tears flowing down my face. When my dad, as an alcoholic, was away from God for twenty-two years, I prayed for him many times. But how many times can you say, "Lord, save my dad who's an alcoholic. Bring him to you"? It went deeper than that. Oh, how beautiful it is when the Holy Spirit touches our human spirits deep within and our need for God that is beyond words goes up to the Lord. Those prayers are powerful and effective. They certainly were for my dad, who came back to the Lord and was set free from alcoholism after more than two decades.

James 5:17 says that "Elijah was as human as we are, and yet when he prayed earnestly that no rain would fall, none fell for three and a half years!" The phrase *prayed earnestly* could be read as "prayed in his praying." We can pray just with our minds, but how much better is a prayer that comes from the deepest part of us and touches the deepest part of God's heart? That's when we see amazing things happen.

A lot of people think that praying, especially when done in public, has to be elegant in its wording. But that's not the kind of prayer God is after. He delights in a Hannah-like prayer that comes from deep within and looks to him alone for the answer. Let's take the words of Psalm 62:8 to heart today: "Pour out your heart to him, for God is our refuge."

Lord, thank you that you're a God I can come to with the deepest needs of my heart. Help me to pour out my heart to you and know that you will hear and answer.

28

MY HELPER

Because you are my helper,
I sing for joy in the shadow of your wings.
PSALM 63:7

Someone has said, "Apart from Christ, pessimism becomes the universal creed." When we're not walking by faith, the world and its negativity can overwhelm and discourage us. In those times, pessimism and unbelief can almost swallow us up. But David, who had problems without number, said to the Lord, "I will praise you with songs of joy . . . because you are my helper" (Psalm 63:5-7).

Satan wants us to lose the ability to say, "You, God, are my helper." Not "You *will be* my helper." Not "You are *the* helper" or "You have helped people in the past." No. We can say, "You, God, right now, today, are *my* helper."

While hiding in the wilderness as people tried to destroy him, David was able to pray, "Because you are my helper, I sing for joy in the shadow of your wings. I know that you're protecting me" (see Psalm 63:7). What wings was David talking about? Where were they? He couldn't see them, but he understood God as his protector. He could have been pessimistic, but he had a spirit that said, "You're my helper. I'm going to sing for joy."

David's men could have pointed out to him, "But your situation hasn't changed yet."

"I know," David would have replied, "but I'm singing for joy because God is *my* helper."

When we lose our confident hope in Jesus, even the best of us fall into pessimism. Satan tries to discourage us by negative facts; bad circumstances; trials and difficulties; a sense that God is not watching over us, is not our helper, has left us all alone. I've had that happen many times. We cry out, "What am I going to do?"

We need to follow the example of George Müller, who could not start the day until he was happy in Jesus, singing for joy in the shadow of his wings. Today let's make it our business to get happy in Jesus. All we have to do is meditate on his unshakable promises rather than focusing on our present circumstances.

Think about the cross of Calvary. Jesus died for us while we were yet sinners! And now that we're his children, won't he help you and me? We cannot consider Jesus' suffering for us and still doubt that the Lord won't come to our aid right when we need it. We should do what the old worship song says: "Think about his love."[7]

I've met some people who are so pessimistic that you feel like you need another conversion experience and water baptism after being with them. But we're not going to live that way today, by the grace of God, because the Lord is our helper.

Another old song says, "Turn your eyes upon Jesus; look full in his wonderful face,"—not on our enemies and circumstances—"and the things of earth will grow strangely dim in the light of his glory and grace."[8] Let's not be negative, glass-half-empty Christians. When we turn our eyes upon Jesus, we will sing for joy in the shadow of his wings. Remember, he's *my* helper and *your* helper this very day.

Lord, thank you that in the midst of my challenging circumstances, you are my helper. I look to you. I know that you will take care of me.

29

GOD'S TENDER HEART

I will win her back once again.

HOSEA 2:14

God's covenant people, Israel, were always turning their backs on God. The northern kingdom, which had separated from the southern tribes after Solomon's death, had become just about as pagan as the Canaanite tribes around them.

God could have said, "All right. You don't want me? Then I'll let your own idolatry bring destruction on you." But no. His incredible love kept reaching out to them, over and over, pleading with them. He continually sent them prophets, warning them, trying to get them to come back. "What you sow, you will eventually reap," God told them. "This will not end well for you."

One of the prophets God sent was Hosea. His book is full of emotional appeals from the Lord. Hosea likened the relationship between God and Israel to a marriage relationship in which Israel was repeatedly cheating on her husband. God's language to backsliding Israel is so tender: "I'm going to win you back. I know you don't want me, but I still want you." What a love!

And that's how God is today with the backslider, the person who has drifted from him or whose heart has gotten cold or hard. God doesn't say, "Oh, all right. It's going to be that way? I'm done with you." No. He tries to win that person back again: "I will lead her into the desert and speak tenderly to her there. I will return her vineyards to her and transform the Valley of Trouble into a gateway of hope" (Hosea 2:14-15).

Perhaps you're not in a good place today in your relationship with Jesus, and your life is not working out the way you thought it would. Trouble is often permitted by God to get us to turn and listen to his tender appeals. He doesn't say, "See what happened? I told you so. You made the mess you're living in." No. In the valley, God tenderly restores our souls. He speaks kindly to us. He turns the valley of trouble into a gateway of hope.

It's so easy to drift from God, like Israel did. In America, with our materialism and pleasure-seeking, Almighty God often loses out to the almighty dollar. Oh, we might regularly attend church on Sundays (although not for too long!). But in our hearts, we stray from God. We spend our time and money following the false idols that bring no peace or fulfillment. Yet God still reaches out to us, saying, "Come back to me. You're on the wrong path." If we listen, we will hear his voice.

Sometimes in the valley of hardship, we get quiet enough to hear what God is saying. We realize that we're not self-sufficient and that we need to return to our wonderful Savior who loves us.

I didn't always live consistently for the Lord, especially in college. Yet at night, after a day of foolishness, I would hear God's voice saying, "What are you doing? This is what you think your life is about? You know better. You once enjoyed fellowship with me." He was trying to win me back. What a wonderful God we have.

Remember, the one who knows us best loves us most, and that's Jesus.

Jesus, you are so kind to keep loving me when I wander from you. Help me listen to your voice and stay close to you. I want to love you with all my heart.

30

GUARDING THE TEMPLE

Don't you realize that your body is the temple of the Holy Spirit?

1 CORINTHIANS 6:19

When the Israelites began returning home from captivity in Babylon, a great many of them were Temple workers. Their task was to rebuild Solomon's famous Temple, which had been destroyed. Among this group "there were 212 gatekeepers" (1 Chronicles 9:22). Who were the gatekeepers? Security people, really. These servants came from a long line of reliable men who guarded the Lord's house on all sides, working in shifts, so that the Temple was kept safe 24-7.

Why was such a large security force needed? Not to protect the altar of sacrifice in the outer court or the furniture inside the Holy Place—the table of showbread, the golden lampstand, or even the altar of incense. Beyond all these things, in the Holy of Holies, above the Ark of the Covenant and the golden mercy seat, was the shekinah presence of God. No one went into the Holy of Holies except the high priest, who sprinkled blood on top of the Ark, his heart beating rapidly. He was in the manifest presence of Almighty God.

That's why Israel had gatekeepers. They didn't want a pig brought in to desecrate the place. They didn't want people stealing things. Everything was watched carefully because the center of life for Israel was the house of the Lord, where the presence of God was. That's what separated the Israelites from all other people—more than circumcision, more than not eating pork. God was literally with them.

Why does the Bible mention so much about this? And how does it relate to us all these years later? The Old Testament Temple was a symbol of God's ultimate intention in the new covenant: "Don't you realize that your body is the temple of the Holy Spirit, who lives in you and was given to you by God?" (1 Corinthians 6:19). Each of us is the temple of the Holy Spirit.

The same Spirit who raised Jesus from the dead dwells in us! How little we think of that. This is probably the least understood truth in the New Testament.

What condescension on God's part that he would dwell in us individually! But that's why we were cleansed through the blood of the Cross—so that the Holy Spirit could come and live in us. That makes our bodies sacred. There's no holy place on earth—no building, no land. God doesn't dwell in a building anymore. Instead, we individual believers are his true temple. His holy presence indwells us.

That's why the Bible tells us to avoid sexual immorality and other wrong things. Sin profanes the temple, where God dwells. We need to act as gatekeepers. May God help us to walk carefully, staying alert and assessing what's happening around us, because Satan wants to desecrate God's temple.

But that's not going to happen. The Holy Spirit enables us to guard his temple: "May your whole spirit, soul and body be kept blameless at the coming of our Lord Jesus Christ. The one who calls you is faithful, *and he will do it*" (1 Thessalonians 5:23-24, NIV). Our bodies are the temple of the Holy Spirit. That's awe-inspiring—and cause for praise. It also means that we are responsible for guarding the temple of Christ.

Thank you, Lord, that you live inside me. What an amazing reality! Help me yield to your Holy Spirit in me so your temple will be sacred.

31

PRAISE FROM GOD

They loved human praise more than the praise of God.

JOHN 12:43

Inside each of us is a desire to be accepted. Very few people want to have the world or their family against them.

People in Jesus' day were no different. The Bible tells us that many of them believed in Jesus, "including some of the Jewish leaders. But they wouldn't admit it for fear that the Pharisees would expel them from the synagogue" (John 12:42).

The Pharisees were self-righteous fundamentalists, not unlike the fathers of today's ultraorthodox Hasidic Jews. They were held in such high regard that the people tried hard to gain their approval. When Jesus began teaching, many rejected him. But some Jews, even some among the leaders, put their trust in him. The Pharisees, however, considered Jesus a heretic and a blasphemer. So, sadly, many who believed in Christ would not openly acknowledge their faith for fear they would be expelled from the synagogue. For a Jew, that was like being sent into no-man's-land.

These "secret believers" weren't willing to go against the flow of popular opinion. They weren't committed enough to Jesus to risk alienation from the religious establishment. They hadn't understood that if they accepted Jesus they wouldn't need the Jews'—or non-Jews'—approval for anything. They would have Jesus. That's all that mattered.

What was at the bottom of their fear? "They loved human praise more than the praise of God" (John 12:43).

But Jesus warned his followers about this: "If you want to be my disciple, you must, by comparison, hate everyone else—your father and mother, wife and children, brothers and sisters—yes, even your own life. Otherwise, you cannot be my disciple" (Luke 14:26).

In America today, we are surrounded by an anti-God culture. We are constantly tempted to keep our identity as believers hidden for fear that people will think, *What, you're a Christian? One of those narrow-minded judgmental bigots?* We know deep down that we don't fit in with the crowd around us.

One of the reasons I wasn't a strong Christian in college was that I wanted to fit in. I was in New England—not exactly the Bible Belt. I was fairly well known on campus because of my basketball playing, and I was afraid of hearing someone say, "Oh, you're one of those Holy Rollers?"

Too many of us care more about getting "likes" on social media than about receiving God's approval. Instead of saying, "I will follow Jesus no matter what," we wonder how we can please our friends or family. But when we base our actions on the approval of others, we lose praise from the one who matters most.

Imagine, Christ gives praise to those who stand for him. That's what today's verse tells us. The apostle Paul said it too: "A person with a changed heart seeks praise from God, not from people" (Romans 2:29).

Let's live today not for the praise of people but for praise from God.

Oh, Lord, I want to care more about what you think than what people think. Help me to understand that when I have Jesus, I have everything that matters.

32

LOVING JESUS

Mary took a twelve-ounce jar of expensive perfume . . . , and she anointed Jesus' feet with it, wiping his feet with her hair. The house was filled with the fragrance.

JOHN 12:3

Jesus liked being around people who loved him. After all, so many people hated him. Imagine how his nervous system must have been affected by people plotting to kill him even as he taught the multitudes. But with friends, he could relax for a while and enjoy fellowship.

One place Jesus often went was the home of Lazarus and his sisters, Mary and Martha. Lazarus was a dear friend whom Jesus had raised from the dead. The Lord had a special love for this family (see John 11:3, 5). Lazarus, Martha, and Mary loved Jesus too, and they showed it.

Martha showed her love behind the scenes in the kitchen, cooking for and serving not just Jesus but also everyone at the house. She often has received a negative reputation since she once complained that Mary wasn't helping her. But Martha loved the Lord, and she demonstrated it by serving. God notices when we serve him: "God is not unjust. He will not forget how hard you have worked for him and how you have shown your love to him by caring for other believers, as you still do" (Hebrews 6:10). When we serve others, we are showing love to Jesus.

Lazarus showed his love to Jesus by simply being with him. He sat with the Lord, reclining at the table, fellowshiping with him. And no wonder. Jesus had brought him back to life. Lazarus hung on every word from the Lord's lips. We can show our love for Jesus just by being with him, having fellowship with him, sharing our lives with him. That's why people get married—they want to be with the one they love.

Mary showed her love through worship. In front of everyone, she took valuable perfume worth about a year's wages and poured it on Jesus' feet. It was the duty of a servant to wash a visitor's feet, which had become dusty from the roads. But Mary didn't use water. She used precious ointment, and its fragrance filled the room. She didn't count the cost. It's like the song says: "When praise demands a sacrifice, I'll worship even then."[9] Those words have stuck with Carol and me. People are never cheap with the ones they love. Never.

One of my first jobs when I was home from college one summer was at a home-improvement business in Queens. When I got my first paycheck, I spent the whole thing buying clothes and jewelry for my girlfriend, Carol.

My mother, a thrifty Eastern European, asked me, "What'd you make? Let me see your check."

"I don't have it."

"What'd you do?"

"I spent it all on Carol."

"The whole thing?"

I didn't care. I was in love.

Let's consider the price Jesus paid when he showed love to us. Then, whether it's by serving others, or spending time with the Lord, or worshiping him in some heartfelt way, let's love Jesus back today.

Lord, make me more Jesus-conscious than self-conscious. I want to serve you, be with you, worship you. You are my everything.

33

STRENGTH THROUGH WEAKNESS

He was crucified in weakness, yet he lives by God's power. Likewise, we are weak in him, yet by God's power we will live with him.

2 CORINTHIANS 13:4, NIV

Believers around the world are all thrilled on Easter Sunday. "Christ is risen from the dead!" We celebrate the message. We rejoice in the fact that the glorified Christ overcame death, hell, and Satan and is now crowned with glory. "Our God has all power!" we say. "He is Lord of all."

But while Jesus rose in strength and "lives by God's power," in order to get there, he had to be "crucified in weakness" (2 Corinthians 13:4). Weakness and death came first—then resurrection.

Just as a seed must be planted and die before it can bring forth fruit (see John 12:24), so it was with Jesus. He could have called ten thousand angels to rescue him from the cross, but he gave way to a humiliating death. He revealed human weakness with a body that experienced thirst, had nails pounded through it, and suffered pain. The path to Jesus' resurrection, power, and glory had to be through the weakness of death on the cross.

What does this mean for us? The second half of 2 Corinthians 13:4 tells us: "Likewise, we are weak in him, yet by God's power we will live with him."

Many of us want to experience God's power so that we can effectively help others. But we can't violate the principle that Jesus himself experienced: First comes weakness—yielding to circumstances that are hard to bear, taking up our cross, denying ourselves. Dying to self involves pain.

Paul and Silas were imprisoned in Philippi—what a sign of weakness. What was Paul thinking when the Philippian authorities were viciously beating him and Silas? The people watching the two missionaries singing and praising God in prison could have said, "Where's your Jesus?" That's what the skeptics said to the Lord on the cross: "Where's your Father? Come down, and then we'll believe."

Holding to the will of God in a position of weakness means *death to self*. This is the only road to resurrection power. But since the Spirit who raised Jesus from the dead lives in us, that same Spirit will give life to our bodies (see Romans 8:11), and God will do extraordinary things through us, weak as we are.

The strongest Christian is, in another sense, the weakest. When Paul was given a thorn in the flesh, he pleaded with the Lord three times to take it away. But God said to him, "My grace is all you need. My power works best *in weakness*" (2 Corinthians 12:9).

Growing up, I thought that the most powerful Christian was a kind of superman who quoted verses and had everything work out for him all the time. He never cried, never suffered, never doubted. But the strongest Christian is more like someone hobbling on a crutch over all kinds of obstacles. It's in that kind of person we see the truth that God's "power works best in weakness."

Let's not try to be strong today. Let's be weak in ourselves and rely totally on the Lord. Then God's power can work through us. When we try to be powerful in ourselves, we end up spiritually weak. But when we are weak—accepting our frailties, denying ourselves, and taking up our crosses—then right around the corner we will discover resurrection power in ways we can't imagine.

Lord, I don't like being weak. But help me die to self so that your power can be displayed in my life—to your glory.

34

TEST YOURSELF

Examine yourselves to see if your faith is genuine.

2 CORINTHIANS 13:5

If you ask someone, "How is it between you and Jesus?" you may hear things like, "Oh, I go to church on Sunday. I own a Bible. And I even read it sometimes. And just the other week, when my son was in a car accident, I asked the pastor to pray. Trust me, I believe in the good Lord."

But God's Word demands that we look a little deeper into our spiritual condition. "Examine yourselves," the apostle Paul wrote, "to see if your faith is genuine" (2 Corinthians 13:5). And that was written to church folk in the city of Corinth.

So how *do* we know if our faith is genuine? Some would say, "Of course I have faith. I believe in Jesus. I believe in the Apostles' Creed. I know that Jesus was born of a virgin, crucified under Pontius Pilate, and raised from the dead."

But that's not how we discover our true condition. "Test yourselves," Paul wrote. "Do you not realize that *Christ Jesus is in you*—unless, of course, you fail the test?" (2 Corinthians 13:5, NIV). The test of genuine faith is whether we know that *Christ Jesus lives in us through the Holy Spirit.* If that's not true of a person, he or she is not a Christian.

We can memorize the entire New Testament. We can hold to five-point Calvinism. We can believe in the gifts of the Holy Spirit. But none of this makes us a Christian. To be a Christian, we have to be born again by repenting of our sins and trusting Jesus as Savior. Romans 8:9 says, “Those who do not have the Spirit of Christ living in them do not belong to him at all.” There it is in plain English.

This is what separates the new covenant from the old. The people of Israel, under the law, had God’s commands. But they chose self, sin, and idols over God, which our fallen sinful nature will always tend to do. The revolutionary thing about Christianity is that God doesn’t just forgive our sins, as wonderful as that is. He actually comes to live within us through the Spirit!

Well-known writer and Bible teacher Warren Wiersbe once said to me, his voice breaking, “You know, Jim, sometimes I think that half the people attending evangelical churches are not born again. They attend out of habit, culture, or loyalty to family. Or they go to offset how they lived during the week.” The vital signs of the new birth, such as loving God’s Word, wanting to be in his presence, and longing for heaven, are rare (see Acts 2:42). Going to church and intellectually accepting the doctrines of the Bible are not the same as being born again.

Let’s examine ourselves. Are we sure beyond a shadow of a doubt that Christ Jesus lives in us through the Holy Spirit? Some people maintain that we can never be sure about that fact. But we can be sure, or Paul wouldn’t have said, “Test yourselves.” Romans 8:16 says that God’s “Spirit joins with our spirit to affirm that we are God’s children.” We *have* to know.

Let’s be sure that Christ lives inside us today. And if he does, let’s rejoice in the fact that we are part of God’s family.

Thank you, Jesus, that being born again means that you live inside me. I thank you for the grace that has made me a child of God.

35

TIRELESS GRACE

We also pray that you will be strengthened with all his glorious power so you will have all the endurance and patience you need.

COLOSSIANS 1:11

Paul had never visited the Christians in Colossae. Why, then, did he write them a letter?

Paul had learned of these believers' faith, so he wrote to them, "We have not stopped praying for you since we first heard about you" (Colossians 1:9). What was Paul praying for? That these believers would experience the power of God—in fact, "*all* his glorious power" (Colossians 1:11). Wow! So they could perform miracles and cast out demons? No. These things are certainly modeled in the New Testament, but Paul's concern was about something even more valuable. He wanted the believers to experience "endurance and patience" (Colossians 1:11).

The Greek word translated *endurance* here means staying strong in trying circumstances. Difficulties are part of the Christian life. The early believers knew that from personal experience. Christians today who are surrounded by hostile populations, as in the Middle East, understand this too. And even those of us living in safer environments often deal with uncomfortable situations that don't seem to change.

The word *patience* means bearing with people—not blowing up at them but continuing to love them even when they are hard to put up with.

The only way to be like Christ in the midst of trials, tribulations, spiritual attacks, temptations, discouragements, letdowns, and opposition is by the endurance and patience available through the Holy Spirit.

The unwearying endurance and patience that God offers us are totally supernatural. They won't fail us in times of trial, since they don't originate with us. When we become testy and impatient with people, it's a sign that we need to stop, humble ourselves, and receive fresh infusions of the Holy Spirit.

When we think of all the suffering Paul went through, it's hard to imagine how he kept a sweet spirit and continued to reveal the love of Christ. I mean, everywhere he went he had problems (see 2 Corinthians 11:22-28). How sad that, for many of us, the least inconvenience sends us into a funk. But Paul had such grace from God that he could say, "We rejoice in our sufferings" (see Romans 5:3).

So how did Paul do that? It's because his mind, heart, body, and spirit were being renewed by Jesus every day. Through the Spirit's power, he became tireless and kept going on, no matter what.

Just like everyone else, I've gotten really tired at times. It's natural to feel that way after a long day of preaching and praying with people. But being tired is not an excuse for being irritable and complaining. Whenever I become that way, I know I've gotten away from my source of strength.

The disciples never had to tell people, "You'd better leave the Lord alone right now. Lots of people are rejecting him today. He heard about them plotting his murder, so he's not in a very good mood." Jesus never ran out of endurance and patience. Never. God's grace doesn't get tired.

Let's drink deeply of God's grace today and keep on drinking. We can't eat a little breakfast and stay full the rest of the day. The Bible encourages us to "walk by the Spirit" (Galatians 5:16, NIV). That means our everyday lives can be controlled by the Holy Spirit's gracious influences. When we stay close to the Lord, we'll find that he will supply all the endurance and patience we need.

Lord, I need you every day, every hour, every moment. Give me grace now to face the problem in front of me.

36

HELP FOR TODAY

The Lord is my helper, so I will have no fear.

HEBREWS 13:6

We all need help. Unfortunately, we don't always understand that God's help is available to us right now, today.

Many of us know from the Bible that God has helped people in the past. He exerted his power when his people called on him because he had promised to help them. And God was faithful to his promise. We also know that one day in the future, the Lord is going to return. He has gone to prepare a place for us, and he'll come and take us to be with him for eternity. There we will have perfect joy and peace in a way that we can't imagine.

But many times we forget what Hebrews 13:6 tells us: "The Lord *is* my helper." It's not "He *was* my helper" or "He *will be* my helper someday in the future." The Lord is our helper *today*.

God has helped us many times with past problems, getting us out of trouble and protecting us even from the results of our own bad decisions. And since "Jesus Christ is the same yesterday, today, and forever" (Hebrews 13:8), we know that we can depend on him for future problems too. But what's important to realize is that we have an invisible helper with us right now.

The Lord delights in helping us. When my kids were young, we had a basketball hoop in our backyard. One day, as I was washing dishes, I noticed through the window that my son was shooting baskets. He was just learning and was having a little trouble. Basketball had been my life in high school and college, so I dropped what I was doing and went outside. "Come here, James," I said. "You've got to follow through." And I showed him how to shoot a basketball correctly. I delighted in helping my son.

How much more does our Lord love to help us? He can't help us in the past—yesterday is over. And tomorrow isn't promised to us. So "the Lord *is* my helper" is the truth we need to remember. We can depend on him today, right now. People who don't know the Lord carry their own burdens and try to figure things out alone. But as Christians, every day when we wake up, we can count on the fact that Jesus is our helper that day.

Because of this, we can say with the writer of Hebrews, "I will have no fear" (Hebrews 13:6). Why will we have no fear? Because there aren't dangerous things in the world? Because we won't deal with surprises in our day? No, we will have no fear because the Lord *is* our helper. He's with us this very moment. He will help us through whatever the day brings.

When we live in fear, we are out of the will of God. That includes worry and anxiety, because Philippians 4:6 says, "Don't worry about anything"—not a single thing. Why? The Lord is with us.

If we haven't asked God for help today, let's do it. Let's not just theoretically count on the fact that the Lord wants to be our helper. We need to engage him, saying, "Lord, help me through this day." And repeatedly, throughout the day, we can say, "Oh, Lord, this problem has just come up. I need your help." He loves to help us.

Let's rejoice in our Lord, who is not only our Savior and God but also our helper *today*.

Lord, you have promised to be my helper today. So I will say with confidence, "I will not worry or fear."

37

FROM ORDINARY TO EXTRAORDINARY

Be filled with the Holy Spirit.

EPHESIANS 5:18

In the early Christian church, God used ordinary people to do extraordinary things. People who had been cowards in the midst of trouble were now bold to preach and even work miracles. Although they had no seminary training or advanced degrees, a small group of fishermen and other common people turned the world upside down.

How?

They were filled with the Holy Spirit.

That was the key. Prior to this transformation, Jesus had discipled these men for three and a half years. But what had it produced? On the night Jesus was arrested, they all ran for the hills, and Peter denied him three times. Was their doctrine wrong? No. What they needed was spiritual power within them.

And that's what they got when they were filled with the Spirit. Jesus had promised, "You will receive power when the Holy Spirit comes upon you" (Acts 1:8), and so it came to pass. Suddenly they were doing extraordinary things, affecting the people around them.

Notice that God purposely used people who had very little natural talent so that all the glory would go to him. God desires to do the same thing with his people today.

So often we hear things like, "Oh, bless your poor little heart" or "I'm not much." But when our "poor little hearts" are filled with the

Holy Spirit, amazing things happen. The question is not how much we've studied, or even how sincere we are. The question is, are we filled with God's power—the same power that raised Jesus from the dead?

We need to ask God for the Holy Spirit—and ask repeatedly. Ephesians 5:18 says, "Be filled with the Holy Spirit." This verse was written to Christians in the church in Ephesus. It could be translated "Keep on being filled" or "Be being filled." This is not about one stop at the gas station. We're to *keep on* drinking in God's Holy Spirit, who will enable us to powerfully fulfill God's will.

For the early believers, that meant spreading the gospel, even though they had a poor track record. Imagine it—Jesus put those men in charge of world missions. That's incredible! The Christian church was built by ordinary people doing extraordinary things. Why? Because their little old hearts and limited credentials were overshadowed by the power of the Holy Spirit.

When I went into the ministry, I battled with insecurity. "Lord, why didn't you let me go to seminary? I believe you called me into the ministry, but why choose a basketball player with a degree in sociology?" I had to get over that and remember what Paul said: "I can do everything through Christ, who gives me strength" (Philippians 4:13).

The great need for each one of us is to pray, and to keep on praying, "Oh, Lord, fill me with your Holy Spirit so I can make a difference for Christ today." Let's ask the Lord. Maybe he has something in store for us that we have never imagined but can experience today. What other day could we have it? It doesn't matter how we've failed or succeeded. Today's a new day. Let's be filled with the Spirit and help others in the name of Christ.

Lord, my lack of credentials or talent doesn't matter to you. Fill me afresh with your Holy Spirit today and every day, and use my life for your glory.

38

WHAT *NOT* TO DO

Gideon said to God, "If you are truly going to use me to rescue Israel as you promised, prove it to me in this way."

JUDGES 6:36-37

When I was growing up, I often heard believers say, "I'm not sure what to do in this situation. I'm going to put out a fleece before God." I had no idea what they were talking about. The way I heard *fleece* used on the street was "That guy fleeced me," as in robbed or swindled. But *fleece* in the Bible comes from something that happened to Gideon, one of the judges of Israel.

We shouldn't read the Old Testament narratives and automatically say, "I need to follow what these people did." Sometimes even the best Old Testament saints made wrong choices. One example is when Gideon put out a fleece.

During a time when the Israelites were being oppressed by the Midianites, the angel of the Lord appeared to Gideon. "Mighty hero, the Lord is with you!" he said. "Rescue Israel from the Midianites. I am sending you!" (Judges 6:12, 14).

But Gideon was afraid. He had all kinds of excuses. So he decided to test God: "I'll put a wool fleece on the threshing floor. If there's dew on it in the morning but the ground is dry, then I'll know you're going to help me." God, in his mercy, condescended to answer Gideon (see Judges 6:36-40). But it was doubt and unbelief that made Gideon use the fleece. God had already told him, "I am with you. Go, mighty warrior!" What more did Gideon need?

Putting out a fleece is like telling God, "Okay, Lord, I know what you said, but it looks impossible to me. So I'm going to put this ballpoint pen on the desk, and if it moves by itself, I'll know you're with me." Oh, God is merciful, isn't he? But he doesn't want us putting out fleeces every other day.

What *does* he want us to do? He wants us to be full of faith in the Word of God and sensitive to the Holy Spirit. Then, when he leads us, we will follow with confidence.

Sometimes discerning the Lord's direction is a delicate matter. The apostle Paul once tried to go into certain areas to spread the gospel, but the Spirit of Jesus forbade him. So he sat still and waited. Then God gave him a vision of a man pleading, "Come to Macedonia," and Paul concluded that God was calling him to go there and preach the gospel (see Acts 16:6-10).

A great missionary statesman I knew was invited to travel to Mongolia. He was up in years, and it would be a tough trip. So for days he prayed, "Lord, is this of you? I'm open, but this is a huge undertaking." One day he was driving and praying, "God, should I do it?" He stopped at a red light and noticed that the car in front of him had a big bumper sticker with the words "JUST DO IT." Seeing that, the Holy Spirit witnessed to his heart. He knew he should go. "Thank you, Lord," he said, and off to Mongolia he went.

Let's not make a habit of throwing out wild things for God to do before we follow the Spirit's leading. Whenever we're not sure, let's pray, "Lead me, Lord," and God will give us the confirmation we need.

Lord, help me to live in your Word and be sensitive to your Holy Spirit so I can know your will. Help me to courageously follow your lead, whatever you ask.

39

DON'T STOP THEM

"Don't stop him!" Jesus said. "No one who performs a miracle in my name will soon be able to speak evil of me."

MARK 9:39

The Bible tells it the way it is. One of the uncomfortable facts it reveals about Jesus' twelve disciples is that they had wrong attitudes and perspectives on a lot of things.

The disciples wanted to keep children away from Jesus because they thought blessing them would inconvenience him (see Matthew 19:13-15). They wanted to call down fire on a village because its people rejected Jesus (see Luke 9:51-55). When they saw a man they didn't know casting demons out of people in the name of Jesus, they forbade him because he wasn't in their group. "Leave the demons in those people," they basically said. "Don't do that in Jesus' name. You're not part of our crowd" (see Mark 9:38-40).

How hard it is for many Christians to be happy about God blessing local churches other than their own!

The spirit of denominationalism is a horrible thing. The Lord doesn't want us to be Baptist, Charismatic, or Reformed. He wants us to be Kingdom people—New Testament Christians. That's why Jesus told the disciples, "Don't stop him! . . . No one who performs a miracle in my name will soon be able to speak evil of me. Anyone who is not against us is for us" (Mark 9:39-40).

We should obey the Lord by rejoicing when other believers rejoice and mourning when they're sad. Jesus prayed that his followers might be one as he and the Father are one (see John 17:21). But God's people, sadly, are divided. The church is not like the National Football League, where it's the Bears versus the Lions. There's only one team, and we're all on it.

When I was in my first year of ministry, an older preacher took me out to lunch. He was one of the few people who would come and preach in our depressing, run-down building. He gave me some very important advice.

"Listen, Jim. You're going to meet three kinds of people among Christians.

"First, you're going to meet people with a local church spirit. '*My* pastor said . . . ' '*My* church . . . ' 'I don't know about that church across town . . .' In other words, for these people, the local church is their only world. It's all they can see.

"Second, you'll meet people with a party spirit—five-point Calvinism, Pentecostalism, Methodism. To them, nobody else exists. When they say 'we,' they won't mean you, Jim. They'll mean only them."

Then he said, "Third, if you're blessed, you'll meet people with a Kingdom spirit. They don't know walls, party spirit, local churches. They're just out for Jesus and the extension of his Kingdom. Wherever the Lord is glorified, they rejoice. Wherever the Kingdom is hurt, they're sad, and they want to pray."

That has come true. The man was prophetic. Sadly, too few people I have met have had that Kingdom attitude.

At that time I started praying, and I still continue today, "God, make me a New Testament Christian who loves the body of Christ." We can be Kingdom people today. Let's break down fences that divide believers in Jesus and hold back the work of God.

God, let me see the body of Christ the way you see it. Let me rejoice with my brothers and sisters in Christ and help them as they do the work of the Lord.

40

LAMBS AMONG WOLVES

I am sending you out as lambs among wolves.

LUKE 10:3

When the Lord sent out his disciples to minister to people, he sent them out "as lambs among wolves" (Luke 10:3). Who were the wolves? People who would persecute and hate the disciples. Even today, many people still resist Jesus.

Jesus sends us out in the same way. He told his followers then, and he tells us today, "If they hated me, they'll hate you. If they persecuted me, they'll persecute you" (see John 15:18-20). But as we get ready to go out into the world, Jesus tells us, "No matter how nasty the wolves are, I want you to be as a lamb."

We see so much meanness today in our anti-Christian culture. If we're not careful, it can make our blood boil. Then things can get personal. But Jesus wants us to submit to God in our circumstances, like the apostle Paul did.

When Paul went into the synagogues, he would spread the gospel to the Jewish people there. Some would believe. Others not only didn't believe, but also spoke abusively to him. Instead of arguing and getting angry, Paul would just move on.

I stayed overnight once at the warden's house in Angola, Louisiana, where the infamous Louisiana State Penitentiary (known as Angola) is located. Angola is a maximum security prison that had more than five thousand inmates at that time. The warden kept two wolves in his front yard. (Obviously he and I had different tastes in pets!) When I arrived at the house, those wolves ran toward me. Thankfully, they were behind a fence, but that didn't keep my heart from beating fast. I wanted to get into the house—quickly.

When I came down for breakfast the next morning, the warden's wife said, "Sit down, Pastor. I made you coffee." Suddenly the side door opened, and the warden walked in with a wolf on a leash! The warden was a strong guy, but that wolf was pulling him. I found it difficult to concentrate on my coffee.

I looked down at the wolf, and it caught my gaze. They say that wolves, like dogs, know when you're scared. It was as if I had texted that wolf, "I'm afraid of you." Suddenly the creature lunged toward me. I was too proud to cry out, "Excuse me, Warden, please get that animal out of the room." Fortunately, his wife said, "Honey, get that wolf out of here. You know I don't like the wolf in the kitchen."

When people we encounter start acting like wolves, our tendency is to say, "I'm going to be a fiercer wolf than you. I'll show you." I've even heard people brag about their harsh reactions, with comments like, "When she said that, Pastor, I went *off* on her."

Well, lambs don't go off on anyone. Jesus said, "I'm sending you out as lambs surrounded by wolves. Don't bite back when people snarl at you. Let me protect you."

Let's trust God and not get nasty when people are nasty to us. We're supposed to be like lambs, as Jesus was when he was arrested. He could have called thousands of angels from heaven and destroyed the people who were after him. But instead, he fulfilled the prophecy, "He never said a word" (Isaiah 53:7). He took the mistreatment and let his Father settle the issue. Let's be like Jesus today.

Oh, Lord, my natural tendency is to fight back when people are nasty to me. Make me like you, Jesus—a lamb among wolves, trusting the Father.

41

GREATER JOY

You have given me greater joy than those who have abundant harvests of grain and new wine.

PSALM 4:7

Many people today believe the lie that the more they have, the happier they'll be. So they look for joy in all the wrong places—money, power, acceptance by their peers. But we discover from reading the news that some of the wealthiest, most high-profile business titans, movie stars, and athletes are the most empty, unhappy people on planet Earth. All their fame, money, relationships, and possessions have not given them joy and fulfillment. In fact, while the culture idolizes them, many self-destruct through wild living.

When David wrote Psalm 4, he was under heavy pressure. People were talking badly about him, accusing him falsely, ruining his reputation. It was the perfect recipe for anxiety and depression. But David, as he so often did, turned to the Lord. "Free me from my troubles," he prayed. "Have mercy on me and hear my prayer" (Psalm 4:1).

David easily could have spiraled down into anger or despair. But as he prayed, he reasoned with himself: "Don't sin by letting anger control you. Think about it overnight and remain silent" (Psalm 4:4).

As David pondered, his heart quieted. Then he remembered the true source of joy: "Many people say," he wrote, "'Who will show us better times?'" But then David thought, *I don't need better days.* He continued, "Let *your* face smile on us, LORD. You have given me greater joy than those who have abundant harvests of grain and new wine" (Psalm 4:6-7).

It's obvious to anyone who observes the people around them that the missing commodity in our culture is this blessing called joy.

Where I live in downtown Brooklyn, there isn't a lot of joy. People are complaining, mad at the government, upset with their families or friends or bosses. Maybe that's why so many turn to substance abuse—they want to escape the reality of their unhappy worlds.

On a recent visit to Eastern Europe, I met a group of Roma people. In the country I visited, the Roma people are strongly discriminated against. (They're usually called by the derogatory name "Gypsies.") Many of them can't get jobs. Their children sometimes aren't allowed to go to school. They live in neighborhoods that are drastically different from others in their cities. Many of the ones who don't know Jesus fall into lives of crime. But the Christian Roma people I met were the most joyful believers I think I've ever been around. These people have very little. Unfortunately, they are looked down on even by some Christians in their country. But they have something most others don't—God-given joy!

God gives joy to people who have faith in him and worship him and find their delight in him. That's why David could boast, "You have given me more joy than people with the biggest harvests." Believers in Jesus should never envy people who have better houses or more money or fame. That is not the road to joy. *We* have the true road to joy. It's Jesus.

Let's stop looking for happiness in all the wrong places. Let's look to God, like David did. Remember, the joy of the Lord is our strength (see Nehemiah 8:10). Let's *enjoy* our relationship with the Lord today, as the apostle Paul challenged us to do in Philippians 4:4: "Always be full of joy in the Lord. I say it again—rejoice!"

I know, God, that houses, cars, money, and friends can never make me truly happy. Only you can fill me with joy! Make me a joyful Christian today.

42

GIVE GOD WHAT YOU HAVE

Jesus asked, "How much bread do you have?"

MARK 8:5

Jesus was teaching huge crowds that followed him and hung on his every word. One day, when thousands of people were gathered in a remote place to hear him, they stayed so long that they ran out of food. So Jesus told his disciples, "I feel sorry for these people. They have been here with me for three days, and they have nothing to eat. If I send them home hungry, they will faint along the way" (Mark 8:2-3).

Now Jesus was tired himself. He also knew that the religious leaders were plotting to kill him; he could feel their visceral hate for him. At the same time, his own disciples didn't really understand what he was about. He was exhausting himself teaching people and healing the sick. Yet he looked at the crowd and said, "Look at them. They're tired. They've come a long way. They're out of food. These folks won't make it back home."

Jesus knows everything we are going through this very day, and he has compassion on us. If he was concerned about the food supply of people in his day, how much more does he care about our hurts, our challenges, the mountains that seem too high for us to get over?

The disciples, unlike the Lord, hadn't noticed the people's needs. But Jesus pointed out the situation, telling them, "They have nothing left to eat" (see Matthew 15:32).

The disciples replied, "How are we supposed to find enough food to feed these people out here in the wilderness?" (see Matthew 15:33).

This is typical of how many of us respond when the Lord gives us an opportunity to minister to the needs of others: "I can't do it. This problem is too big for me." We say, "I'm too young." "I'm too old." "I haven't been properly trained." "I'm too shy." "I don't know enough Bible verses."

Then Jesus asked the disciples, "How much bread *do you have*?" (Mark 8:5).

"Seven loaves," they said.

Seven loaves of bread to feed thousands of people seemed preposterous. That's how Satan wants us to look at ourselves when we're faced with human need. He whispers, "You don't have what it takes." But it doesn't matter how little we have if we give it all to Jesus.

Personally, I am limited in many ways. I'm not super talented. But I have learned that if I surrender what I have to him, Jesus will bless and multiply it.

So Jesus took the seven loaves of bread, along with a few small fish. Then, after telling the people to sit down, he thanked God for the food. How good it is to thank God for what we have, even when it seems inadequate to meet the challenge.

Before Jesus had the disciples distribute the loaves, he broke them. Let's remember, whatever God blesses, he breaks. We all tend toward pride and are too self-reliant. But when we give Jesus what we have, he breaks it and reminds us, "Yes, I'll feed the people through you. But whatever I bless, I break. Only broken vessels can be used by God."

Let's give what we have today to the Lord. It's not about what we have. It's about what Jesus can do with what we have.

God, I don't have much, but I give it to you. Break it and bless it, and use it to minister to others, in Jesus' name.

43

THE REAL DEAL

Pure and genuine religion in the sight of God the Father means caring for orphans and widows in their distress and refusing to let the world corrupt you.

JAMES 1:27

Martin Luther was a larger-than-life figure whom God used in 1517 to initiate the Protestant Reformation. He stood alone against an entire corrupt religious system that taught salvation could be found only through good works and the Roman Catholic church. God had revealed to Luther from Scripture that we are justified in Christ alone, by grace through faith, so he proclaimed it courageously, even under threat of death.

Because Luther so treasured God's grace through faith, he never took much of a liking to the book of James. What James wrote is not a theological treatise, like Romans or Ephesians. It's made up almost completely of practical teaching—how a Christian should live every day.

Many people think this is because James, whom most scholars agree was the half brother of Jesus, grew up with our Lord. James had seen the perfect way Jesus lived at seventeen, twenty-two, twenty-five. James looked at the nominal believers of his day and saw that they in no way resembled his brother Jesus. "Wait a minute," he said. "That's not true Christianity. I saw the genuine article. When Jesus comes into your life, you'll live differently."

So James stuns the casual believer with his definition of true Christianity: "Pure and genuine religion in the sight of God the Father means caring for orphans and widows in their distress and refusing to let the world corrupt you" (James 1:27).

"Orphans and widows." Who are they? They are vulnerable people. The have-nots. In the Old Testament, they were actually God's secret second "chosen people." Israel was the people of the covenant, but the Lord spoke often of widows, orphans, and foreigners. God warned the Israelites, "Do not take advantage of those people or cheat them in their wages, because if they cry to me, I will hear them and come to judge you" (see Exodus 22:21-24; Deuteronomy 24:19-22). And some of these people who were so special to God weren't even descendants of Abraham, Isaac, and Jacob!

This is exactly the same spirit in which James taught. If we see people who are weak, vulnerable, and suffering and don't care about them, then we'd better check ourselves and see if we're really believers. We are all called to reflect God's compassionate heart.

True religion, James added, is also "refusing to let the world corrupt" us. James was assuming—before the internet, before pornography, before Broadway and Hollywood—that the world will automatically contaminate us if we're not careful. It will soil our garments, pollute our thinking, degrade our speech, and mess up our values. To James, the idea of a worldly Christian was an oxymoron. He was saying, as John did elsewhere, "No, no. If you love the world, you don't have the love of the Father in you" (see 1 John 2:15).

We don't naturally have hearts for vulnerable people. Neither do we have what it takes to keep ourselves unstained by the world. But with God all things are possible. Let's ask the Spirit of God to give us the heart of Christ. Then we will have compassion for people. And we will be able, by God's grace, to remain unspotted by the corrupt world around us.

Lord, I want the real deal. Give me the heart of Jesus so that I will reject the ways of this world and instead love and care for the vulnerable, like you do.

44

SACRIFICES THAT PLEASE GOD

Let us offer through Jesus a continual sacrifice.

HEBREWS 13:15

In the Old Testament ritual of worship, people were to bring physical sacrifices—grain for thank offerings, animals for sin offerings, etc. The sacrificial system was elaborate. All the adult men were to appear in Jerusalem three times a year, and they were not to come without an offering to give.

When Jewish people left this system and were born again in Christ, they faced being ridiculed by their fellow Jews. "What kind of religion do you have?" observant Jews might have said. "It's all invisible. There are no sacrifices, no magnificent temple, no special order of priests. You've got a bunch of untrained fishermen teaching you!" Some Jewish believers were tempted to go back to Judaism—to the Temple, the sacrifices, the priests, all the religious pomp and ceremony.

But the writer of Hebrews told them, "Don't go back. We have a *better* covenant than Old Testament Israel. We have Jesus. He's greater than Moses, greater than the high priest. He himself is the sacrifice, given once for all so we can have our sins forgiven and become part of the family of God."

Then the writer encouraged the Jewish Christians even further. As followers of Jesus, he wrote, they *did* have sacrifices they could bring to God: "Let us offer through Jesus a continual sacrifice of praise to

God, proclaiming our allegiance to his name. And don't forget to do good and to share with those in need. *These are the sacrifices* that please God" (Hebrews 13:15-16).

One of the sacrifices Christians can give to God is praising the name of Jesus every day. With overflowing hearts we can praise the Lord, even out loud when possible. Each day we live, we should have hearts filled with praise.

Some would say, "Oh, but I do praise God! Every Sunday morning from 11:00 to 11:18 during the singing time at my church."

But Hebrews says, "No, continual praise! Every day."

In 2024 I was in Slovakia, and I watched a game of football—what Americans call soccer. When Slovakia beat Belgium in their round at the Euro Football Championship, you would have thought it was New Year's Eve in the stadium. Everyone was yelling and screaming. No one was embarrassed. And for what? A soccer match that nobody will remember ten years from now. Let's never be ashamed or shy in using our voices to praise God and confess the name of Jesus.

Another sacrifice we can bring the Lord is "to do good." We can do good today. How about saying an encouraging word to someone? Everyone needs that. Or how about taking someone out for lunch? We can give a person a glass of water, a cup of coffee, a kind word, a prayer.

We can also sacrifice to God as we "share with those in need." We can help people who are hurting financially. Or maybe we know people in need emotionally, who grew up with no love in their homes. We can share with them the joy and peace Jesus has given us. We can express love toward them and come alongside them.

God is pleased when we offer these kinds of sacrifices. Wouldn't we want to make him happy after all he's done for us? It's so easy to bring a sacrifice to the Lord Jesus Christ. It's in our mouths, in our hands, and in our wallets. Let's do it today.

Jesus, you have done so much for me. Help me sacrifice to you from a heart overflowing with praise, goodness, and a desire to share with others.

45

WHEN TO WALK AWAY

Don't follow the path of evildoers. . . .
Turn away and keep moving.

PROVERBS 4:14-15

When the people of Israel asked for a king, God gave them Saul. Saul started his reign well but ended up full of himself. When someone is full of the devil, demons can be cast out. But when a person is full of himself, it's an entirely different problem.

Saul was impatient and carnal. His public image was everything to him. What God felt about things was secondary. After David slew the giant Goliath, Saul gradually became morally insane with jealousy. He spun out of control, trying to kill David, the very man who had saved him and his people.

Toward the end of Saul's life, the Philistines came to attack Israel. When the king saw the vast army, he was filled with fear. He asked God what to do, but because he had rejected the Lord, the Lord refused to answer him. So Saul went over the edge and consulted a witch for guidance!

The next day, "the Philistines closed in on Saul and his sons, and they killed three of his sons—Jonathan, Abinadab, and Malkishua" (1 Chronicles 10:2). King Saul died later the same day. What a terrible end for this man who had been anointed by the prophet Samuel when the people demanded a king.

But here's what's even more heartbreaking: Jonathan, Saul's son, had been David's best friend. He would have been secretary of state when David became king. When Saul railed against David, Jonathan always defended his friend. Based on that, it's a tragedy that godly Jonathan fell in a battle that Israel had no chance of winning since God was no longer with them.

Sadly, Jonathan lost his life fighting the wrong battle for the wrong person. Yes, Saul was his father, but spiritual dynamics are stronger than blood. When God has turned on somebody because that person has turned on God, why risk our lives fighting battles that God has never called us to fight?

When a drive-by shooting or fentanyl death occurs, we say, "The poor guy was only twenty-four. He died needlessly. What a shame." But what a shame that Jonathan died fighting a battle with a father who had just consulted a witch.

People sometimes remain in a church that, for whatever reason, God has ceased to bless. Why? Maybe a grandmother attended there, or maybe they were baptized there years before. Now they're dying on the vine and spiritually dry. We must remember that our loyalty is to Jesus alone.

Let's not get involved with battles God never called us to fight. The Lord didn't call us to fight culture wars. Fighting the world's battles will produce anger, and we'll lose out with God.

We all need wisdom for this. Some things we should join and give ourselves to fully. When God calls us to a church or ministry, we should get behind it financially, prayerfully, practically. Other things are clearly wrong—people denying Christ, preaching another gospel. Those are battles we need to fight. Then there are things we're unsure about that possibly don't bear witness with our spirits, like someone asking us to give money for a cause we're uncertain about. Probably in those cases we just need to "turn away and keep moving" (Proverbs 4:15).

Let's ask God for wisdom to know when to join something, when to fight, and when to walk away.

God, it's easy to be loyal to the wrong things. I want to be loyal to you. Show me who to join and which battles to fight—and when to walk away.

46

JOYFUL WORSHIP

David danced before the L*ORD with all his might . . . with shouts of joy.*

2 SAMUEL 6:14-15

David was a worshiper. He treasured the presence of God. But the Ark of the Covenant, which was central to the worship of the Lord in Israel, was not in the sanctuary of God where it needed to be. So David, after becoming king, had a deep desire to bring the Ark back to where it belonged.

Years earlier, the Ark had been captured by the Philistines in a battle with Israel. When the people of Israel got it back, they placed it in the home of a man named Abinadab, where it stayed for twenty years (see 1 Samuel 7:1-2). Above the Ark were two cherubim, or angelic figures, where God's presence was to dwell and meet with his people. *I can't settle down as king,* David thought, *while the symbol of our covenant with God is somewhere else.* So he made arrangements to move it.

The day the Ark was returned to Jerusalem was a great celebration. David had musicians playing and choirs singing. People were rejoicing—blowing rams' horns, crashing cymbals, playing loud harps. David didn't wear his kingly garments; instead, he wore a linen robe, as the Levitical priests did. He was singing and dancing, skipping and laughing joyfully. This wasn't emotionalism—David was worshiping freely from his heart. This is what made David so special to the Lord. With David, what you saw was who he truly was. And it was pleasing to God.

David's wife Michal, who was Saul's daughter, wasn't so pleased. "When she saw King David skipping about and laughing with joy, she was filled with contempt for him" (1 Chronicles 15:29). When David came home that night, she said to him, "You made a great fool of yourself out there. Instead of wearing your kingly robes and being politically correct, you were acting like a child" (see 2 Samuel 6:20). But David didn't care, nor was he embarrassed. He would continue to worship the Lord with all that was in him.

Today we can be like David or like Michal. We can worship God and rejoice the way David did. This doesn't mean getting carried away into emotionalism. That doesn't profit anything, and it's not pleasing to God. Real worship is a sincere expression of love for God from deep within us. Or we can be like Michal and criticize those who show sincere emotion as they praise the Lord freely.

Scripture tells us that Michal was barren and childless for the rest of her life (see 2 Samuel 6:23). Isn't that all too true of believers and churches that get excited about almost everything but Jesus? They rarely bear fruit or win souls for Christ.

What was David so happy about? God had taken him from tending sheep and made him king. Now he was overseeing the Ark of the Covenant's return to where it belonged. What do we have to celebrate? How about the fact that all our sins are gone? That we're born again? That our names are written in the Lamb's Book of Life? That when we die, we're going to spend eternity with Jesus? David wasn't aware of these truths, yet he worshiped God with all his heart and soul.

Let's imitate the believers found in the book of Acts, who were "filled with joy and with the Holy Spirit" (Acts 13:52). No wonder. They knew Jesus! Let's worship God freely today and be happy in the Lord.

Oh, Lord, let me not be inhibited in my worship of you! Let my love for you overflow in a joyful and free expression of praise.

47

A NEED FOR WISDOM

If you need wisdom, ask our generous God, and he will give it to you.

JAMES 1:5

Just because we're Christians doesn't mean we are wise.

I graduated from college with a degree in sociology and a minor in philosophy. Then, in a path I never expected to take, I ended up in the ministry. I realized early on that I didn't have the spiritual wisdom of a brick. Boy, did I make some terrible decisions. Did I mean well? Did I love the Lord? Was I willing to make some sacrifices? Absolutely. But possessing wisdom, no.

We can be sincere believers in the Lord Jesus Christ—reading our Bibles, serving in our churches—yet because we lack wisdom, we can also hurt ourselves, our marriages, our children, our work, our finances.

James told us what to do when we lack wisdom: "If you need wisdom, ask our generous God, and he will give it to you" (James 1:5). This is what made Solomon so special at the beginning of his reign, when God offered him *anything* he wanted. "No, God," he said, "I'm not asking for wealth or the death of my enemies. Give me a wise heart to rule the people, because I'm young and inexperienced" (see 1 Kings 3:5-9).

When the early church was choosing deacons to hand out food to the widows, the disciples told the people to "select seven men who are well respected and are full of the Spirit and *wisdom*" (Acts 6:3). This was a requirement not only for pastors, but also for the men who organized the food distribution. We certainly need wisdom in the church, and we also need wisdom in our personal lives. And the good news is that God wants to give it to us.

As I grew in the Lord, I learned that I could conduct a church service wisely or unwisely. I could preach a sermon wisely or unwisely. I began praying, and I still pray to this day, "God, please give me the wisdom I need."

My wife, Carol, not only is gifted musically, but she also possesses the spiritual wisdom needed to write and arrange songs that connect with people. When she writes, she chooses chords and music that match the lyrics being sung. As the Bible tells us, wisdom builds the house (see Proverbs 9:1).

When I was about fifteen, riding the subway one day in New York, a lady on my train car was witnessing to people. She went from person to person. When she came to me, she leaned right over me. I couldn't help but look at her. She had bad breath, and she screamed at me, "You're going to hell! Do you know that? You're going to hell!" She did that to every person. Now the Lord did promise, "You will be my witnesses" (Acts 1:8), but I'm not sure that's what he had in mind. This lady had no lack of zeal, but she sure lacked wisdom.

Let's start today, and every day, by asking God to give us wisdom. We can live today with wisdom or without it. But as James said, if we ask God for it, he will give it to us.

God, grant me wisdom for my day, my family, my ministry, my job, my interactions with unbelievers. Give me the bountiful supply you have waiting for me.

48

GET SOME REST

Jesus said, "Let's go off by ourselves to a quiet place and rest awhile."

MARK 6:31

Jesus had sent out the disciples to minister in his name. They had gone into different environments, some more hostile than others. They had preached the gospel, cast out demons, and healed the sick. When they came back and reported to the Lord everything they had done, Jesus realized what was best for them: "Let's go off by ourselves to a quiet place," he said, "and rest awhile" (Mark 6:31).

My late friend Warren Wiersbe once said to me, "Listen, Jim, sometimes God's perfect will for us is to take a nap."

I recently read an article that said the new scourge harming especially young people is sleep deprivation. People are staying awake to scroll social media or surf the internet. So they end up not sleeping enough. Studies show that this behavior makes a person much more susceptible to diseases, negative reactions, and even reduced brain activity.

The Lord has a practical word for all of us today: We need to ask him for wisdom to know when to get away for a while to a quiet place and rest. Everybody needs an occasional vacation. That is why God instituted the Sabbath in the Old Testament for Israel. Remember, rest is what the mighty prophet Elijah needed (see 1 Kings 19:3-6). Both his nerves and his body were worn out.

When I was in college, a guy in our dorm either stayed up till three or four in the morning and got two or three hours of sleep, or he went to bed and got a normal night's sleep. The next day everyone knew which one it was.

Rest is important because our spirits can be affected by our physical condition. When we are physically fatigued, we can make bad decisions, have a harder time resisting temptation, or fly off the handle. A great promise in this regard is found in Psalm 127:2: "God gives rest to his loved ones."

As a young pastor, I saw God beginning to bless our church. But with the pressure of ministering in the inner city, not having much money, and then our oldest daughter getting away from us and the Lord, my nerves got so bad that at one point I cried every time the phone rang. Often more activity under stress produces less tranquility, less peace, less poise. Sometimes we need a greater balance between activity and rest, especially if we have type A personalities or a rushed pace of life with many responsibilities.

This probably means getting honest about our cell phone use. Sometimes I wonder how it's possible to find a quiet place unless we throw our phones into the Hudson River! Being addicted to our phones and using them as a stimulus keeps a lot of us from the physical and emotional rest we need.

The most important aspect of finding rest, though, is to start the day alone with God in a quiet place. It calms our nerves. It renews us inwardly and reminds us of how big God is, and then our problems don't seem so overwhelming anymore. Our nerves might get worn thin, but we can maintain our spiritual poise by getting away with the Lord. Let's do it today.

God, I need rest. Help me stop all the motion and come away with you to a quiet place. Thank you that you give rest to your loved ones—including me.

49

TREASURING HUMILITY

He leads the humble in doing right,
teaching them his way.
PSALM 25:9

When I was at Erasmus Hall High School, a guy I knew named Jerry could *really* play basketball. He was a gifted athlete. But he also had an attitude. No one was going to tell him anything. He tried out for the varsity team the same year I did, and we both made the team. One day we were practicing foul shots, and the coach said to him, "Hey, Jerry, you've got to pull your elbow in when you shoot."

Jerry didn't like that. "Who said? That's what *you* think. Other guys can shoot that way. I shoot *my* way," he said. To the coach!

Jerry was gone the next day.

God, our heavenly Father, wants to teach us. He loves us. But many of us who believe in him miss out on his teaching. Why? Because the Lord "leads the *humble* in doing right, teaching them his way" (Psalm 25:9). Without a spirit of humility, we can't be taught.

James writes, "God opposes the proud but gives grace to the humble" (James 4:6). The Greek word for *opposes* gives the idea of a general or king, in this case God, in full battle array with his whole army to bring down an adversary. Wow! It's not a pretty picture when the Almighty stands against you.

But God "gives grace to the humble." To be a good student in the school of Jesus Christ, the requirement is not vaccination shots or transcripts from your previous school. It's humility, childlike simplicity, dependence on a loving Father.

Those who know it all can't rely on God. They live independently of him. How many of us are held back by know-it-all-ness? The Lord wants to pour out understanding and wisdom on us, but our lack of humility keeps us from receiving it.

Why is God so dead set against pride? Some commentators have said it might be because it reminds him of the great rebellion in heaven when Lucifer, the most beautiful of all his angelic creations, was lifted up with pride (see Isaiah 14:12-15). Even though no devil yet existed to tempt him, pride was his downfall. And it came from the very beauty that God had bestowed on him. That's the destructive power of pride!

Paul taught Timothy, "When you ordain leaders, don't appoint a new believer, because he is young and hasn't yet realized who he is. He could become proud and come under the same judgment," or "doom," one translation says, "of the devil" (see 1 Timothy 3:6, CEV).

True humility shouldn't come only from our sense of sinfulness and failing God. Yes, sin is a humbling thing, as we see in Psalm 51, written after David's downfall. But the person who had the most humility in the world was Jesus Christ, and he had no sins to humble him. Real humility is emptying ourselves and depending on our Father for everything, just as Jesus did. That's what all of us need today.

The devotional writer Andrew Murray said that humility is "the root of every virtue."[10] God has ordained that his blessings flow through the channel of humility. And it's also the prerequisite for being taught by God. The Lord will teach us, but we need the humility that says to him, "I need thee, oh, I need thee."[11]

Lord, I want to be taught by you. Help me to treasure humility, emptying myself and depending fully on the Father for everything I need.

50

BRING GOD YOUR NEED

My God will meet all your needs according to the riches of his glory in Christ Jesus.

PHILIPPIANS 4:19, NIV

One of faith's biggest battles is learning to believe that God will supply all our needs.

Sometimes our needs seem too big a mountain even for God. Jesus told us, "I will never fail you. I will never abandon you" (Hebrews 13:5), yet we struggle to believe that he will supply in a miraculous way. On the other hand, some needs seem too small or unimportant to even pray about. We think, *The utility bill is overdue.* But we never stop to ask the Lord about it, thinking it's too menial. As I once heard someone say, "God has given us a crown, yet we will not trust him for a crumb."

God permits needs to arise in our lives so we can learn to rely on him and see his faithfulness. Without the test, we can never have a testimony.

One day, before I was married, I had plans to take my future father-in-law and my pastor at the time to lunch. I greatly admired them both. Taking them out was a special treat for me.

At the time, I was working in the business world. Halfway through the morning, I realized that I didn't have any cash on me. I also didn't have any credit cards. Just as I realized my predicament, my assistant brought in a travel reimbursement report for a business trip I had taken. Suddenly the thought came to me, *I have no money, but I can easily get money. I'll just fudge this report and get an extra hundred dollars.* It was for a good cause, after all—I was taking out two ministers! But the Holy Spirit convicted me. *No, I cannot do that.*

So I prayed, "God, I'm going to trust you. If I have to be humbled and say, 'Gentlemen, I'm sorry. I promised you the meal, but I can't buy it,' then that's the way it will be."

At lunchtime I went to the elevator bank, where a group of people stood waiting. The elevators were tied up. So I did something I hardly ever did: I decided to take the stairs to the lobby. I expected to face my future father-in-law and my pastor and apologize for not being prepared.

The stairwell had two levels—a half-flight, a landing, and another half-flight. As I got to the landing, I looked down, and I saw two fifty-dollar bills on the floor! I looked around. If someone had dropped the money, I wanted to give it back. But there was nobody above. Nobody below. I reached down and picked up the money. I knew that God was showing me that even for a lunch for two ministers, he could supply my needs.

Since then I've had to believe God for multiplied millions of dollars. But the God who gave me that hundred dollars is the same God who can supply millions.

Maybe today you're going through a test. God wants you to have a testimony. So don't be overwhelmed by what confronts you. Step back and see the big picture: "My God will meet all your needs" (Philippians 4:19, NIV). Our Father is going to take care of his children.

Today let's trust that the one who has promised us a crown will also give us the crumbs.

God, give me today my daily bread—and whatever else I need. I know you will give me a testimony of your faithfulness as I learn to trust you.

51

DEVOTED TO PRAISE

And 4,000 will praise the Lord.

1 CHRONICLES 23:5

When David was old, he appointed his son Solomon as king over Israel. David had provided all the materials for Solomon to build the Temple, and now he wanted to give his final instructions. So he summoned all the leaders of Israel, including 38,000 Levites. Then David said, "From all the Levites, 24,000 will supervise the work at the Temple of the Lord. Another 6,000 will serve as officials and judges. Another 4,000 will work as gatekeepers." Then he said something unexpected, but important: "And 4,000 will praise the Lord with the musical instruments I have made" (1 Chronicles 23:4-5).

In any construction project, we see the need for supervisors. We understand needing arbitrators to settle discrepancies, arguments, and legal matters. We also certainly recognize the value of gatekeepers, like the security force David appointed to guard the gold, precious stones, and other valuables for the new Temple. But why assign four thousand valuable people to do nothing but praise the Lord?

Notice how important praise was to David! God delighted in David because David delighted in God so much. Half of the psalms in the Bible were written by David, often during severely dire straits. But his overriding concern, which we see over and over, is that God would be praised. As he wrote in Psalm 107:31, "Oh that men would praise the Lord!" (KJV).

So David assigned four thousand Levites to do nothing but praise the Lord. They weren't to pick up a brick, a stone, or a piece of fabric. Their job was just to keep praising God, thanking God, worshiping God.

We should do nothing for the Lord without the spirit of praise. That's why Philippians 4:6 says, "Do not be anxious about anything, but in every situation, by prayer and petition, *with thanksgiving*, present your requests to God" (NIV). Even in bringing our worries to the Lord, the direction is given, "You've got to mix thanksgiving with it."

On Sunday mornings in many of our so-called worship services, there's probably not a whole lot of heart worship. We sing some praise and worship songs, but too often it is not full-hearted, full-throated. It's done in a mechanical manner. I'm not sure David would feel so comfortable in many of our churches.

Some believers do praise the Lord wholeheartedly in church. But praising God with a "Hallelujah" on Monday morning while driving to work is not the ordinary pattern for many of us. We need to remember what Hebrews 13:15 tells us: "Let us offer through Jesus a *continual* sacrifice of praise to God."

Years ago, when I was in Alabama, I went to my first Waffle House. One of the Waffle House's claims to uniqueness is that they're open 24-7, 365—even on the holidays. What if we became worshipers 24-7, 365? How it would please the Lord and open the windows of heaven!

We don't have to live in a monastery to praise the Lord continually. You could be a doctor doing surgery and be praising God in your heart. We can praise the Lord wherever we are. God inhabits the praises of his people. Let's praise him today—all day long.

God, I don't praise you enough. Teach me to lift my heart and my voice in praise to you on Sundays and every day of the week.

52

DETERMINED FAITH

What do you want me to do for you?

MARK 10:51

Large crowds were following Jesus. He was famous for his teaching with authority and the incredible miracles he performed. As he and a large entourage were leaving Jericho one day, they passed a blind beggar named Bartimaeus sitting by the road.

This man had never seen the Lord, of course. But he had heard of Jesus of Nazareth. So when he realized that Jesus was passing by, he cried out, "Jesus, Son of David!" He knew that Jesus was not just another teacher. Somehow he'd had a revelation that Jesus was the Messiah. "Have mercy on me!" he shouted.

But as in most cases when we're trying to believe God for something great, there was opposition. The crowd didn't think this man's shouting was proper for such a noted teacher. "Hush up!" they told him. But because of his persistent faith and his deep desire to receive a miracle from Christ, Bartimaeus cried out even more.

When we're believing God for something in prayer, we need a stick-to-itiveness, a fervency, a determination that nothing is going to stop us. Sometimes the enemy suggests, "It's too late. Forget it. It's impossible." But nothing deterred Bartimaeus. He just yelled louder.

When Jesus heard Bartimaeus's cries, he stopped dead in his tracks. When someone full of faith is crying to the Lord, fighting through opposition, Jesus is going to give that person his attention. He said, "Bring him to me."

When the beggar reached Jesus, the Lord spoke to Bartimaeus with these wonderful words: "What do you want me to do for you?" (Mark 10:51).

If Jesus said that to a blind beggar who hadn't been walking with him but somehow knew that he was the promised Messiah, why wouldn't we think that Jesus is asking us the same thing today? "What do you want me to do for you?"

"No, that's too good to be true," you might say.

But God loves us. We're his children. Why wouldn't he want to help us with what we need? I'm not talking about selfish, crazy requests like "I want a loaded Rolls-Royce." I'm talking about honest requests that would bring glory to God.

The blind man answered Jesus, "I want to see."

Jesus said to him, "Go, for your faith has healed you" (Mark 10:52).

It wasn't the beggar's yelling that healed him. It wasn't his boldness. Jesus healed him because of his faith.

"Anything is possible," the Lord said, "if a person believes" (Mark 9:23). He didn't ask the man, "Are you worthy?" He didn't say, "Maybe I can help you." No, he said, "Believe." Yes, it was Jesus who healed the man, but Jesus also said, "Your faith has healed you."

As soon as the man could see, "he followed Jesus down the road" (Mark 10:52). Happily, this wasn't the end of the story. "Thank you, Lord," he said, and he became a true follower of Jesus.

What do you need today? What's holding you back? What heartaches are you carrying—a wayward child, a physical problem, a financial need? There is nothing we can't bring to Jesus of Nazareth, Son of David, Messiah, Son of God. Let's believe him today. The person who trusts Jesus will never be disappointed.

How amazing, Lord, that you care about what I need. Give me the boldness of blind Bartimaeus to cry out to you, no matter the opposition, and believe that you will answer.

53

OPEN DOORS AND OPPOSITION

There is a wide-open door for a great work here, although many oppose me.

1 CORINTHIANS 16:9

Paul and Barnabas, on Paul's first missionary trip, were traveling from town to town on the island of Cyprus. When they reached Paphos, the governor, Sergius Paulus, invited them to come and tell him about Jesus. What an incredible open door for the gospel. Paul and Barnabas were so happy. "Look what the Lord has done. The governor *wants* to hear us!"

But Sergius Paulus had an advisor named Bar-Jesus who was a sorcerer and false prophet. When Paul and Barnabas started explaining the gospel, Bar-Jesus didn't like it. "Don't listen to these men, governor," he said.

How could such opposition suddenly block a door that God had opened?

Paul and Barnabas could have said, "We thought this was an open door from God. But look, Sergius Paulus respects this guy. What are we going to do now?"

But they didn't get discouraged. Instead, what happened next was sensational. Paul "was filled with the Holy Spirit, and he looked the sorcerer in the eye. Then he said, 'You son of the devil, full of every sort of deceit and fraud, and enemy of all that is good!'" (Acts 13:9-10). Now "son of the devil" is not something most pastors or evangelists typically call people. But it goes to show us that God's ways are not our ways.

Paul went on, "Watch now, for the Lord has laid his hand of punishment upon you, and you will be struck blind" (Acts 13:11). Suddenly Bar-Jesus began groping around, begging for someone to lead him.

When God opens a door for us, we *will* face adversaries. That's a given. It's like Paul later experienced in Ephesus: "There is a wide-open door for a great work here, although *many oppose me*" (1 Corinthians 16:9). But when opposition comes, God will show us what to do, just as the Holy Spirit showed Paul that God would judge Bar-Jesus on the spot.

When the governor saw the authority and power connected to the gospel, he said, "Sign me up!" What Satan had done to block Sergius Paulus from hearing the truth, God used to win the governor over to Christ!

The Protestant reformer Martin Luther was no stranger to open doors and opposition. He, along with William Tyndale and other church reformers in the sixteenth century, began to preach something that had been lost for centuries: "You can't earn salvation. It's only by the grace of God." The printing press had been invented in the mid-fifteenth century, so for the first time, God's truth could be widely published and spread abroad. What an open door!

But opposition? The whole world stood against Martin Luther. The pope, along with the entire religious system, called him a wild boar that needed to be hunted down and killed. But God protected Luther, and untold numbers of people were saved as the truth of salvation by grace through faith in Christ alone spread throughout the world.

Many times God has opened doors for Carol and me, and adversaries have come against us to discourage us. But when opposition has come, we have learned that if we rely on the Holy Spirit, he'll show us what to do. Not only that, but the very opposition we have faced has turned out to glorify the faithfulness of God.

Thank you, God, for open doors. Help me not to be discouraged by opposition but to listen for your guidance and believe you for powerful eternal results.

54

ETERNAL PERSPECTIVE

Then I went into your sanctuary,
O God, and I finally understood.
PSALM 73:17

The author of Psalm 73 had a major problem. He was a godly man, set apart for the Lord, yet he had almost lost his spiritual footing.

This man had looked at the wicked and become puzzled and discouraged (see Psalm 73:3-12). "Look, they don't have any troubles. They're proud, they're cruel, they boast, they mock God—yet they have everything their hearts could wish for!"

The psalmist had kept his heart pure, yet he had "nothing but trouble all day long" (Psalm 73:14). "What's going on?" he said. "I've tried to walk in God's ways. And there's no reward. There's nothing. On top of that, God is convicting and disciplining me. But these people who curse God are strutting around like they own the world."

Life, in our short seventy, eighty, or ninety years here on earth, often doesn't make sense. John the Baptist had his head cut off. The apostle Paul was beaten, imprisoned, and shipwrecked. Christians are sometimes destitute or persecuted. And the ungodly people? They prosper and mock Christians. When we try to figure it all out, we can become disillusioned, and our faith is challenged.

But then the psalmist got alone with God. He stopped looking at the physical world around him. And suddenly he received a new perspective: "Then I went into your sanctuary, O God, and I finally understood the destiny of the wicked" (Psalm 73:17). God gave this man spiritual vision: Those who reject God are actually sliding toward destruction (see Psalm 73:18-19).

Once the psalmist understood God's ways, he admitted to the Lord, "I was so foolish and ignorant. But I still belong to you. You will guide me to a glorious destiny" (see Psalm 73:22-24).

We often look on the surface of things and say, "Where's the justice?" But we'll never find fairness here on earth. There is a Judge, though, who will make everything right in the end. Our reward is in heaven.

Some people in the church today falsely teach that wealth is a sign of God's blessing. But the truth is, the richest people in the world are overwhelmingly ungodly and reject Jesus. I've counseled many who were ready to lose their faith because life wasn't working out according to the simple formulas that some Christians are touting. But we can't measure where we are with God by our bank accounts. The real way to measure spiritual growth is by love (see 1 Corinthians 13).

Do we sometimes have material blessings? Can God make a Christian a millionaire who blesses other people? Of course. But we need to remember what Paul and Barnabas said: "We must suffer many hardships to enter the Kingdom of God" (Acts 14:22). And God has chosen the poor to be rich in faith (see James 2:5).

Let's not be discouraged by what seems unfair in the world and complain, "It's not right!" Of course it's not right. But God will soon make it right.

If we're troubled today by the way godless people prosper, we need to get alone with God and wait in his presence. When the Holy Spirit opens our eyes, we won't see only the temporal world around us with all its unfairness. No, we will see the end of the story and what God has prepared for us through Jesus Christ.

Lord, it's hard to see wicked people flourishing, but you will put everything right. Help me stay close to you.

55

PRAYING PEOPLE

All the believers devoted themselves . . . to prayer.

ACTS 2:42

The besetting sin of most churches and Christians is probably prayerlessness. Our faith is weak when it comes to believing God's promise that he is a prayer-answering God. Or, if we do pray, we don't stay at it. "Things haven't changed as I expected," we say. "I've got to go to plan B."

The early church was a praying church. Jesus had taught his disciples, "My house will be called a house of prayer" (Mark 11:17, NIV). Many Christians today prioritize teaching, but the church was not born in a teaching session. It was born in a prayer meeting. The great need today is for people who will spend time with God and pray.

What can prayer do? As E. M. Bounds, a Civil War–era preacher, said, "Prayer can do anything that God can do."[12] Prayer links us up with Almighty God. That's why James wrote, "The earnest prayer of a righteous person has great power and produces wonderful results" (James 5:16).

Satan will do anything he can to discourage us, distract us, and convince us that we'll never be praying people. Why? Because when a Christian or a church prays, God will eventually appear on the scene and manifest his power and grace. This is as sure as day follows night. It's a divine law found in the Bible.

How few Christians actually have living communion or contact with God on a daily basis! Even at church, most of us *say* prayers, like I did growing up, but have little or no true communion with the living God. We fail to "pray through" (see Luke 18:1-8) so as to receive answers from the Lord.

Satan isn't bothered by shallow or carnal Christians. It's true that Satan doesn't like us attending church. But he doesn't mind us going if the church is not a house of prayer. The people he fights against most are praying people.

The day things turned around at the Brooklyn Tabernacle was the day God met me on a fishing boat in Florida, where I had gone to rest for a bit. I was very sick. I had no money, no doctor, and no insurance, so I was hoping that the sun would beat the bronchitis out of me. Truth be told, I needed some time alone with God. I was very insecure about my preaching, and with the meager offerings the church was getting, finances were a major concern as well.

As I prayed on the deck of that boat, I felt the Lord say, "If you and Carol will lead the people to pray, I'll give you every sermon you need. I'll supply all the money you need. And you'll never have a building large enough to hold all the people I will send."[13]

This was no extrabiblical revelation. The fact that God honors sincere prayer is found throughout Scripture and in the testimonies of countless believers over the centuries.

Let's break out of any habit of prayerlessness we've gotten into. Let's do what Jesus told us to: "You should always pray and never give up" (see Luke 18:1).

We all struggle with life's issues and often feel sorry for ourselves. That will change nothing. We are called to be more than conquerors. But we will be victorious only if we are people who regularly call on the name of the Lord.

What can our prayers do? Whatever *God* can do—because praying in faith links us up with the power of Almighty God.

Lord, help me to be a praying Christian!
I want to believe your promise that you
are a prayer-answering God.

56

DON'T PLAY FAVORITES

My dear brothers and sisters, how can you claim to have faith in our glorious Lord Jesus Christ if you favor some people over others?

JAMES 2:1

In India, someone from a high or middle caste cannot traditionally marry someone from a lower caste. It's just not done. Yes, they're both human beings. But the caste system cannot be broken.

Our culture has something like a caste system. We don't call it that, but the people who are the wealthiest, the most beautiful, or the hippest get favors. Or we show partiality to people who are like us—the same color, same culture, same nationality—even when we don't know the content of their character. Anyone who is different from us, we tend to avoid.

This, unfortunately, happens in churches too. Christ died for everyone, but many congregations don't really want certain folks attending who are destitute or a minority or not in the right age bracket. "You know, if you're not in our target group of eighteen through thirty-two," some say, "we're really not the church for you." What a horrible thing.

James, the half brother of our Lord, wrote, "My brothers and sisters, do not show favoritism as you hold on to the faith in our glorious Lord Jesus Christ" (James 2:1, CSB). When somebody rich comes into our churches, if we say, "Hey, here's the best seat in the house," but to a poor person we say, "Stand over there. Ushers, just hide this person, will you, please?" our motives are actually evil (see James 2:2-4).

Being like Christ means not showing favoritism. One of Jesus' friends was Simon the leper. I don't think any Pharisee had a friend named Simon the leper. The religious leaders of Jesus' day wanted to be with the wealthy and the experts in the law. But the common people? Not so much.

Favoritism is not an innocuous thing. "Listen to me, dear brothers and sisters," James wrote. "Hasn't God chosen the poor in this world to be rich in faith?" (James 2:5). Isn't it amazing that God has chosen *poor* people to be rich in faith? Being rich in faith doesn't mean making more money.

I once was in a poor part of Lima, Peru. I had preached my heart out through an interpreter, and people had come forward for prayer. So I went from one person to another, laying my hand on their foreheads or shoulders and praying for them. As I moved down the line, I reached out to the next person—and recoiled. In front of me was a street vendor who looked like she hadn't washed her hair in weeks. She was sweaty and dirty. She had a baby on her back, wrapped in a filthy blanket strapped around her middle. She was weeping, with her hands raised. Everything about my middle-class New York City upbringing kicked in. I stood frozen in my nice suit and tie.

Then I felt the Holy Spirit's conviction. "What? You can't touch her? You were lost in your trespasses and sin. Your righteousness was like filthy rags. Yet I reached out to you."

God broke my proud heart. I put my hand firmly on the woman's sweaty head, and I started praying for her.

Holy Jesus touched lepers, and yet we're drawn to only the rich and influential. Let's take Paul's words from Romans 12:16 to heart today: "Don't be too proud to enjoy the company of ordinary people."

Lord, help me not to favor certain people over others. Help me today to see every person the way you do and to love them.

57

BRING YOUR FRIEND TO JESUS

They couldn't bring him to Jesus because of the crowd, so they dug a hole through the roof above his head.

MARK 2:4

When Jesus went home to Capernaum, many people gathered to hear him teach. Soon the house where he was staying was filled to overflowing. It was standing room only.

As Jesus preached, four men arrived carrying a paralyzed friend on a mat. They had faith that if they could just get their friend into the presence of Jesus, he would be healed. But when they tried to get into the house, they were turned away. "Sorry," they were told. "It's packed."

These men could have said, "Oh, man. I guess that's it. Well, we tried." But instead of giving up, they did something crazy: They climbed up on the roof, dug a hole, and lowered their friend on his mat right down in front of Jesus.

Don't we need that kind of faith today? This very day we may have some mountain in front of us. We've tried to get to Jesus with our problem, but we've run into obstacles. So had these four guys. But they found a way to overcome them.

When Jesus saw a man descending from the ceiling and dangling in front of him, he didn't say, "Guys, the roof! You're tearing it apart!" No. He saw the faith of these four men, and he said to their paralyzed friend, "Your sins are forgiven" (Mark 2:5). Then he said, "Stand up, pick up your mat, and go home!" (Mark 2:11). The man immediately got up and walked out in front of everyone. "We've never seen anything like this!" the crowd said.

How did all this happen? Yes, it was by the power of Jesus. But it wouldn't have happened if four people had not said, "We've got to get our friend to Jesus."

Paul wrote to Timothy, "Pray for all people. Ask God to help them; intercede on their behalf" (1 Timothy 2:1). Intercession is when one hand touches God in prayer, and the other hand touches a person who is in need of God. It's not praying for ourselves. It's praying for other people we know about and believing that God can solve their problems, save their souls, and heal their bodies.

Do you know someone who's hurting or in a real mess today? You could feel bad for that person. Or you could judge the person and say, "It's your fault this is happening to you." Or you could bring that person to Jesus in prayer.

Notice, when Jesus saw "*their* faith"—the faith of the four men—he healed their friend. Who knows what the man himself was thinking. *Why do you have me up on a roof? Why are you dropping me through this hole? Who's down there?* But the *friends* knew that with God, nothing is impossible.

Bringing someone to Jesus might take some doing. We might have to loosen a few tiles in our lives—overcome a habit of prayerlessness, deal with a negative attitude, stir up fresh faith to believe God for an answer. But we've got to take the time to get into God's presence and bring that mother, father, sister, brother, friend to Jesus. There's no telling what God will do when we pray with faith and bring that person into the presence of Jesus.

Lord, I bring my friend or family member to you. The need seems impossible, but you are able. Give me faith to intercede, no matter the obstacle.

58

"AND PETER"

Go, tell his disciples and Peter, "He is going ahead of you into Galilee."

MARK 16:7, NIV

Three women were making their way to Jesus' tomb. They were bringing spices to anoint the Lord's body for burial. On the way, they wondered who would roll away the heavy stone for them at the entrance of the tomb.

But when they arrived, they were surprised to find that the huge stone had already been moved aside. Not only that, but inside the tomb was an angel dressed in white. The women were alarmed.

But the angel said, "Don't be afraid! Jesus isn't here. He's alive! Go and tell his disciples and Peter, 'He is going ahead of you into Galilee'" (see Mark 16:6-7). The news seemed too good to be true.

But notice who the women were to give this news to: "his disciples *and Peter*."

Peter was the one who had told Jesus at the Last Supper, "I'll never desert you. Not me." The other disciples had said it too, but Peter had been the most vocal.

"Not only will you leave me," Jesus had told him, "but you'll also deny me" (see Mark 14:27-31).

When a rooster crowed right after Peter denied the Lord for the third time, just as Jesus had foretold, Jesus looked right at Peter (see Luke 22:54-61). Can you guess the kind of look he gave him?

Well, it wasn't a look of anger. It wasn't a "See, I told you so" look. That's not who Jesus is.

No, it was a look of compassion, from eyes filled with mercy.

Peter went out into the night and broke down and wept (see Luke 22:62). He could have been thinking, *I'm ruined. I went too far. I even boasted that I wouldn't do it.* The devil must have piled on the guilt, accusing him, "You denied the Lord *three times*. The third time you even cursed! God is done with you for sure."

How many times have we felt like that? We fail the Lord, and we're sick with ourselves. We're heartbroken. Then the devil comes and says, "It's over. I mean, look what you've done."

That's why "and Peter" should mean so much to us. Jesus didn't say "and James" or "and Matthew." No, he said, "Tell the disciples *and Peter*."

When Satan tells us it's all over, it's not. We might feel as if we aren't accepted and can't be blessed by God. But that's not true. God is full of mercy and grace toward us. We have to believe that he delights in mercy (see Micah 7:18). God is still saying today, "And Jim, and Carol, and ______________, I'm alive, and I love you. I know what you've done, but I'm going to pick you up and clean you off."

When we let people down, sometimes they give up on us and turn away. But Jesus *never* throws us away, does he? He's the God of the second chance, the two hundredth chance, the two thousandth chance. No one will be strutting around in heaven with their head held high, saying, "You know why I'm here? Look at the wonderful life I've led!" Instead, we will all proclaim for eternity, "Worthy is the Lamb."

Thank you, God, that we serve a Jesus who says "and Peter." If it wasn't for your mercy, where would I be? I love you, Lord.

59

INTO THE PROMISED LAND

"Let's go at once to take the land," he said. "We can certainly conquer it!"

NUMBERS 13:30

"No way," ten Israelite spies said. "Yes, the land is flowing with milk and honey, just like God said. But we can't go in and possess it as Moses says."

God had led the people of Israel out of slavery in Egypt. He had guided them to Mount Sinai, where he had given them the law and instructed them concerning how to worship him. But when they reached Kadesh Barnea, twelve men went to spy out the Promised Land. The faithless report of ten of them caused an uproar in the camp.

"They've got big cities with huge walls," the ten spies told the Israelites. "There are giants there. We've been slaves for generations! It's impossible."

The other two spies, Joshua and Caleb, had a different attitude: "Let's go at once to take the land," they said. "We can certainly conquer it!" (Numbers 13:30).

But the people listened to the ten. "Why is the Lord taking us to this country only to have us die in battle?" they cried to Moses. "Our wives and our little ones will be carried off as plunder! Wouldn't it be better for us to return to Egypt?" (Numbers 14:3).

This is an example of why democracy doesn't work when it comes to spiritual matters.

God was so angry with the people's unbelief that he said, "Those people will never enter the Promised Land! But the children they were so worried about? They'll grow up and go into the land. Joshua and Caleb will go in too, because they had a spirit of faith" (see Numbers 14:21-24).

What is this Old Testament story teaching us today?

When we become Christians, we are delivered from "Egypt"—a life of slavery to sin. God, through Jesus Christ, brings us out of that bondage into a place of freedom. The problem is, some of us today are out of Egypt but not in the Promised Land.

The Promised Land is sometimes seen as a type, or symbol, of heaven. But it can't be heaven, because the Israelites had to fight battles in the land and conquer the idolatrous inhabitants who lived there. No, possessing the Promised Land is a picture of living in the will of God for our lives. It's possessing the beautiful plan the Lord has for each of us, even though there are spiritual enemies to overcome.

As the Israelites wandered in the desert for forty years, did God provide food for them? Absolutely. Did he lead them by the cloud and fire? Yes, he did. But were they where God wanted them? No.

Let's not be like those who were brought out of Egypt, fed and led by God, but never entered into all the Lord had for them because of the "I can't" of unbelief.

When I was growing up, I saw some relatives of mine serving Christ with hearts on fire for the Lord. But as the years went by, instead of possessing everything God had for them, some of them stopped short, and, sadly, some even drifted back to Egypt.

If we're out of Egypt, then we're not what we used to be, praise God. But let's not stop short of the goal set before us. Let's walk forward by faith today and possess everything God has for us.

Lord, I don't want to miss your will. Give me faith like Joshua's and Caleb's that says, "Let's go at once! With the Lord, we can certainly conquer the land!"

60

THE BEST IS YET TO COME

Do whatever he tells you.

JOHN 2:5

The New Testament records two great sayings of Mary, the mother of Jesus.

When an angel came to her and said, "You're going to have a baby without knowing a man," Mary responded, "I am the Lord's servant. May everything you have said about me come true" (Luke 1:38). What amazing faith is revealed in these words.

The other great thing Mary said, decades later, was at a wedding she was attending with Jesus and his disciples. When the wine ran out, Mary looked at Jesus and then told the servants, "Do whatever he tells you" (John 2:5). Because she said that, a miracle happened.

So what did Jesus tell the servants to do? "Go fill these huge jars with water."

"Uh, we don't need water," they could have said. "It's *wine* we ran out of."

Sometimes Jesus directs us to do things that don't make sense on the surface. But he has reasons and plans unlike ours. We need to remember Mary's words to the servants: "Do whatever Jesus tells you."

This means, first and foremost, doing whatever Jesus tells us in the Bible. When the Lord says, "Don't steal," "Don't live an impure life," or "Don't have racial prejudice," by God's grace, we need to say to him, "Today I want to obey your commands."

We also need to do whatever Jesus tells us through the subtle whispers and promptings of the Holy Spirit. "Fill the jars with water" is not a general command found anywhere in the Bible. That was a specific word to the servants at the wedding. It's the kind of word the Lord gave Paul when he told him to stay in Corinth: "Don't be afraid! No one's going to hurt you here" (see Acts 18:9-10). Paul stayed, even though he had previously endured much persecution for the cause of the gospel. He did what Jesus told him to do.

One of the fallacies of modern-day Christianity is that obedience to the words of Christ is an optional thing. Maybe we'll obey, or maybe we'll just follow our own preferences.

When the servants did what Jesus told them, the water miraculously turned into wine. When the master of ceremonies tasted it, he said, "Wow, in most weddings, they bring out the best wine first, and then when everybody's feeling happy, they bring out the cheaper stuff. But you've saved the best for last" (see John 2:9-10).

Notice, this miracle wouldn't have happened if Jesus hadn't been invited to the wedding. Jesus doesn't barge in where he's not invited. We will always see the Lord work on our behalf if we keep on inviting him into our lives, including into every relationship and the decisions we all face daily.

Too many times we become discouraged when we face critical shortages, and instead of consulting Jesus, we listen to the voices around us claiming our attention. Let's invite Jesus to walk with us today, and then we too will say, "He saved the best for last."

God, I invite you into my day, my decisions, my relationships. Help me to do whatever you tell me to do. I know it will bring great blessing.

61

EASY TO UNDERSTAND, HARD TO DO

Do everything without complaining and arguing.

PHILIPPIANS 2:14

Many verses in the Bible are hard to understand.

In the Old Testament, we wonder how Moses talked with God as a man talks with a friend when the Bible says that nobody can see God. In the New Testament, we puzzle over the symbols in the book of Revelation. What is the white horse, the black horse?

Then there are passages in the Bible that are as simple as two plus two equals four. *Obeying* them, though, is another thing altogether. Philippians 2:14, written to the believers in Philippi, is one of them: "Do everything without complaining and arguing."

This verse is plain. It has no secret meaning in the original Greek. We get what it means. But how do we live out what the Holy Spirit is saying in this Scripture?

Most of us don't go a day without complaining or arguing about something. If our latte from Starbucks is too hot, a lot of us grumble about it all day long. I've never met a married couple that hasn't experienced some disagreements. And in many ways, the basic spirit of social media is to complain and argue. In fact, the internet is filled with outright hostility toward other people.

Throughout history, a lot of Christians have majored in disputing instead of spreading the gospel to unbelievers. They also haven't walked together in love. Instead of sweet prayer and fellowship, many would rather argue: "My denomination is better than yours. My doctrinal position is superior." If you don't agree with them, things can turn ugly.

When Paul was ministering, he debated, presented truth, and showed from the Scriptures that Jesus was the Messiah. But the moment people got loud, contentious, or abusive, he would leave. "If you reject my message of salvation through Jesus, I'm moving on to others who need to hear." He confronted people in love, but he wouldn't argue.

Jesus didn't argue with people either. His disciples bickered among themselves about who was the greatest. The Sadducees argued with the Pharisees on doctrinal points. But Jesus went about doing good, never arguing.

If we were facing death on the cross and discovered that the disciples were arguing about who was the greatest, wouldn't it be natural to grumble and say, "God, this is what you gave me? How about a different twelve followers to work with?" But the Lord never complained.

"Do everything without complaining and arguing" is a command from God. And when God gives a command, he always offers the grace to obey it. He doesn't say, "Don't complain or argue. Just do your best to obey." No. The verse right before this command says, "God is working in you, giving you the desire and the power to do what pleases him" (Philippians 2:13).

By the grace of God, let's do everything today without complaining and arguing. Remember, today is our only life. Yesterday is gone, and whatever complaining and arguing we did, we can't take it back. And it's no good to promise, "God, tomorrow I'll stop grumbling." No, today is the day. May God give us the grace we need not to complain or argue.

Lord, I don't have what it takes not to grumble or argue, but you do. Give me the grace to be like you, never complaining or arguing.

62

RUNNING TO GOD

You are my hiding place.

PSALM 32:7

We've all been given instructions about what to do if we're in danger.

When I was in grade school, the Cold War between the Soviet Union and America was going strong. Our teachers told us what to do in case of a nuclear attack—jump under our desks. We actually practiced doing that.

Carol and I were in San Diego once for a music conference. After I spoke, I went up to our hotel room, while Carol stayed downstairs to listen to some of her music being performed. As I was watching the news, suddenly the room started shaking. But I remembered what to do in an earthquake: "Run to the doorframe and stand in it." So I did, along with a bunch of other people up and down the hallway.

We've all thought about where to run in case of a physical emergency. But many of us give very little thought about where to hide when our souls are under attack.

When guilt is pounding at the door of our hearts and Satan, the accuser of the brothers and sisters, is coming at us, we need protection. I once counseled a woman who'd had several abortions decades before she became a believer. "I thank God for salvation," she told me. "But sometimes the enemy just comes and bombards me with, 'Look what you did back then. You think God's going to accept and bless you after all that stuff?'"

Or maybe we're worried and fearful after stepping out into something God has called us to do. "It's not going to work out," the devil whispers to us. "You'll never be successful in what you think God wants you to do."

This is where David, the psalmist, helps us. He knew where to go when his soul was in trouble. He wrote to the Lord, "You are my hiding place; you protect me from trouble" (Psalm 32:7).

Sometimes God being our hiding place means he will provide protection from physical danger. Still, the New Testament recounts saints being persecuted, thrown in jail, and beaten up. Jesus warned us that in this world we would have "many trials and sorrows" (John 16:33). But David was saying that when our souls are overwhelmed or our spirits just crushed, God's presence becomes a place where we can run and hide.

God is a spirit, not a place. But to the psalmist, God's presence was a place where he could go and be surrounded by the consciousness of God's love and faithfulness. "You surround me with joyful shouts of deliverance," he wrote (Psalm 32:7, CSB). In God's presence he found his rest.

Today, as we read this devotion, let's remember that there are not just physical places to run to when we're in trouble. We have a God we can run to. He is our hiding place. When his presence surrounds us, he not only grants us spiritual poise, but he also strengthens us to resist the devil's accusations. We can say no to fear. "I resist you, Satan," we can say. "Jesus said he would never fail me. My Lord will never abandon me."

When we find shelter in God's presence, we will end up rejoicing in the very circumstances that drove us to seek God as our hiding place.

God, when my soul is in trouble, help me to remember to run to you, my hiding place. Quiet my heart in your presence so I can sing for joy.

63

NEW ISN'T ALWAYS BETTER

I am not ashamed of this Good News about Christ.

ROMANS 1:16

One word that the public is fascinated by, and that advertisers exploit, is *new*. Politicians run on a new day, a new era, a new beginning, and people say, "Yeah, I'm so tired of the same old, same old. Let's move on to something new."

We think new means better. And sometimes it is. But not everything that's new is better. In the spiritual realm, something promoted as new can bring disaster.

In our walk with Christ, we have to be very careful about anything called "new." The gospel is the only message of salvation given by God to planet Earth and the lost people living on it. Adding anything to it will lead us toward danger.

"Come on, you're not stuck with that old stuff," someone might say. "What are you, a dinosaur? It's a new day." It might be a new day, but there's nothing new under the sun when it comes to the things of God. As someone once said, "If it's new, it's not true, and if it's true, it's not new."

We can go *deeper* in the things of God. We can have new *discoveries* in the Word of God. But the danger of false prophets, whom the Lord warned us about, is that they don't come saying, "I want to wreck your life and drag you down to hell with me." That's not usually their approach. Instead they say, "God is doing a *new* thing." But if this "new thing" isn't mentioned in the Bible, it's not true.

Paul warned the believers in Galatia, "If anyone preaches any other Good News than the one you welcomed," that is, a new message, "let that person be cursed" (Galatians 1:9). Very strong language.

This fascination with the new is always with us. "What? You're wearing that? That's so passé." We've got to have the newest clothes, the newest energy drink, the newest phone.

What if someone said, "You know what? I'm tired of that sun. It's 93 million miles away, and every single day, it's the same sun. I mean, can we get something new?" But if we do away with the sun, we do away with life. Thank God that the sun is there every day! All the light bulbs in the world won't come near to doing what the sun does. The sun is old, but it's necessary to sustain life on earth.

Whenever we hear of any hot new take on Scripture, we ought to stop and think. If human nature has not changed, why should we think the gospel message should change? The problems Jesus saw in human beings two thousand years ago are the same problems we have today—loneliness, sin, guilt, anger, bitterness, and estrangement from God. Unforgiveness eats us up, and carnal desires bring pain and destruction. The gospel that Jesus gave us—to repent of our sins and believe in him—is the only gospel that can save us.

Let's not be ashamed of the gospel. "It is the power of God at work, saving everyone who believes" (Romans 1:16). That is good news indeed.

Lord, thank you for your never-changing gospel. Like the sun, it's not new, but without it, we'd be lost. Help me love your gospel more than any claim of something new.

64

ROCKY GROUND

Since it didn't have deep roots, it died.

MARK 4:6

Jesus liked telling parables—stories about the physical world that represent spiritual truths. One of his most famous parables was about a farmer sowing his seed.

Some of the farmer's seed landed on rocky ground. That didn't mean the soil had chunks of rock in it. Rather, there was a layer of rock under the ground. In other words, the soil was shallow. The seed sprouted, sure enough. But when the hot sun beat down on the plant, "since it didn't have deep roots, it died" (Mark 4:6).

What does this mean for us? As Jesus told his disciples, the seed is the Word of God. The ground represents people's hearts. And the sower is whoever sows the Word—a preacher, a teacher, a parent (see Mark 4:14).

Jesus explained that the seeds sown on rocky ground represent people who hear the Word and "immediately receive it with joy" (Mark 4:16). This is not a case of someone who rejects the gospel. This is rather a person who hears the good news about Christ and says, "Sign me up! I want to spend eternity in heaven with the Lord. I want my sins forgiven. What an offer of mercy and grace!" There is life springing up from the seed sown. There is even spiritual growth.

But the ground of this person's heart is shallow. Just like a natural plant, the roots go down, but they are blocked by the rocky layer below the soil. So the person trusts in Christ for a while, but his or her faith is short-lived. When trouble or persecution comes because of the Word, this person immediately falls away.

People say that God's Word can do anything. That's true. Its potential is amazing. But here Jesus taught that salvation and spiritual growth also depend on the ground of our hearts. I've seen people so happy to start serving the Lord. And then they realize, "You mean God wants me to change the way I handle money? And I have to turn away from racial prejudice and forgive those who have hurt me?" Folks with shallow hearts don't last in God's Kingdom very long.

When I was in junior high, I wasn't very interested in spiritual things. But a girl named Betty at my church, who was about my age, stood out to me. She loved God so much. While I was wondering, *When will this meeting end?* Betty was at the altar, tenderly praying to the Lord. Unfortunately, when she went to high school, she started to like boys who weren't Christians. She knew she shouldn't be with them, but she couldn't say no. "Bad company corrupts good character" (1 Corinthians 15:33). For Betty, God's Word lost out to the guys she liked, and she fell away from the Lord. Her roots weren't deep enough.

Some people would say that a person like that was never a Christian in the first place. But Betty truly loved God. Sooner or later, problems and persecution will come to all of us. Then we'll find out how receptive our hearts are to the seed that was planted in us.

Yes, God's Word is powerful. But let's pray that our hearts will be good ground (see Ephesians 3:17). Then, when we hear the Word, we will welcome it "and produce a harvest of thirty, sixty, or even a hundred times" (Mark 4:20) what was planted.

Lord, give me a soft, tender heart, and let my roots go deep. Let your Word produce an abundant harvest of fruit in my life.

65

RESTING IN WHAT WE KNOW

This salvation was something even the prophets wanted to know more about.

1 PETER 1:10

In the Old Testament, men of God prophesied things from the Lord that they couldn't see in detail. So they diligently searched, wondering, *When will Messiah come? What kind of deliverance will he bring?* (see 1 Peter 1:10-11).

When God, however, revealed to the prophets that "their messages were not for themselves" but for a later time (1 Peter 1:12), they were able to rest content. They didn't have perfect clarity, but they understood that God had a plan and that his Word would eventually come to pass.

We should learn not to be embarrassed when we don't understand certain portions of the Bible with absolute clarity. For example, I personally lack certainty about some things found in the book of Revelation. How God will work everything out in the future is something I have questions about.

The Christian church has brought ridicule upon itself over the years with various teachings from "prophecy experts." During World War I, the Kaiser was the Antichrist. "Take that to the bank," people said. "Christ's coming is around the corner." Then came the Depression of the 1930s. "This is the third horse of Revelation 6. The end is now." When Hitler tried to exterminate the Jews during World

War II, so-called experts said, "Surely *this* is the end." But Hitler eventually committed suicide. The war ended. The world wasn't over. The end had not come.

Here's what we can be absolutely sure of: We're all going to physically die one day (see Hebrews 9:27)—unless Christ comes back first—and then believers will be with Jesus forever and ever. Those who don't know the Lord will spend eternity in pitch-black darkness, with "weeping and gnashing of teeth" (Matthew 8:12). But believers will receive their eternal reward. No temptation, no tears, no struggles—forever. *That* we are sure of.

When the disciples asked Jesus, "Is this when you're going to restore the kingdom to Israel?" he told them, "It's *not* for you to know the times or seasons that the Father has decided" (see Acts 1:6-7). The angels rejoice more when one sinner repents than when we argue about secondary doctrinal and prophetic issues.

It is valuable to study prophecy, because it's part of the Bible. But if we're not sure what a particular Scripture means, we shouldn't be afraid to admit it and move on to more important matters, like building up Christ's Kingdom. Let's stand on the Rock, Christ Jesus, who said, "Trust in God, and trust also in me" (John 14:1). Isn't that enough? When the prophecies of Scripture finally unfold, *then* we can say, "Oh, that's what that verse meant. I see now."

Let's rejoice today in what we do know: Jesus is our destiny. We're going to be with him for eternity. Until then, we'll face difficulties and spiritual warfare. But let's hold on to the words of Revelation 22:20: "Amen! Come, Lord Jesus!"

God, help me avoid heated biblical debates with other believers. Help me instead to stand fast in what I do know—that I'll spend eternity in heaven with you! I rejoice in that today.

66

LOOKING TO JESUS

We must keep our eyes on Jesus.

HEBREWS 12:2, CEV

King Joash started his reign well. He repaired the Temple of the Lord, which had been ravaged by idol worshipers. He tore down the altars of Baal. This young man swept Judah clean of all its abominable idolatrous practices. His story is compelling reading (see 2 Chronicles 23:16–24:14).

Where did this young king get such strong convictions?

Joash's father had died when he was a baby. His wicked grandmother, Athaliah, had proceeded to annihilate the royal heirs so she could be queen. But what Athaliah didn't know is that Joash's aunt, Jehosheba, had hidden the young prince away. For six years Joash had been protected in the Temple by Jehosheba and her husband, Jehoiada the priest, while Athaliah ruled the land (see 2 Chronicles 22:10-12). During those years Jehoiada had taught young Joash the law of God. When the boy reached seven years old, Jehoiada arranged to proclaim him king. He did it with the required pomp and ceremony. He also had the military put an end to wicked Athaliah (see 2 Chronicles 23:1-15).

So Joash had been blessed, during his childhood and the early years of his reign, with Jehoiada's godly teaching and oversight.

Then, unfortunately, Jehoiada died.

Soon after, the princes of Judah bowed down before King Joash and said, "You're not going to stay with the ways of that old priest, are you? I mean, the guy was prehistoric in his thinking! It's a new day. Jehoiada was just 'God, God, God; the Word, the Word, the Word.' You've got to be open to new ideas."

Unfortunately, Joash listened to these men. "They decided to abandon the Temple of the LORD, the God of their ancestors, and they worshiped Asherah poles and idols instead!" (2 Chronicles 24:18). As long as his mentor had been there for him, Joash had served God. But as soon as Jehoiada was gone, the king walked away from the Lord.

We probably all know people whose godly parents prayed for them and kept them on the right path, but when Mama died, it was "Bye-bye, God. Bye-bye, Bible." Or we've known others who almost make their pastor an idol. They love his eloquent expositions of Scripture. Then the pastor moves to another church or dies, and the people say, "I don't like this new guy. I'm done with serving the Lord."

When Joash turned away from God, a prophet named Zechariah came to warn him. Guess who Zechariah was? The son of Jehoiada the priest, who had watched over Joash when he was vulnerable and young. But when Zechariah prophetically announced to Joash, "You have abandoned the LORD, and now he has abandoned you" (2 Chronicles 24:20), King Joash repaid Jehoiada for his loyalty by killing his son!

Our faith, obviously, must not depend on any relative or friend. We should never so admire a pastor's ministry that we don't develop our own walk with Christ. As much as the Lord might use men and women, they're just flesh and blood. Our devotion should be only to the Lord, lest we turn "to the right or to the left" (Joshua 23:6).

Today let's make sure that we are "keeping our eyes on Jesus, the champion who initiates and perfects our faith" (Hebrews 12:2). Then, whatever else comes or goes, we will stand fast in the Lord.

Lord, thank you for the godly people you've used in my life, but help me never to rest my faith on them. I want to fix my eyes on you alone.

67

RENEWED DAY BY DAY

Our spirits are being renewed every day.

2 CORINTHIANS 4:16

The greatest Christian who ever lived is the apostle Paul. Even though he was not one of Jesus' original twelve disciples, the book of Acts is mostly about Paul and his ministry. He also wrote a good part of the New Testament. What made this man, who tradition tells us was short and not particularly attractive, so extraordinary?

Paul's ministry was powerful, yet it involved a lot of peril. He was "pressed on every side by troubles," "perplexed," "hunted down," and "knocked down" (2 Corinthians 4:8-9). None of us can imagine what Paul went through physically and emotionally. But Paul's troubles didn't destroy him. No. Instead, Paul wrote, "We never give up" (2 Corinthians 4:16). He was something like a kamikaze for Christ.

The Japanese kamikazes almost turned the tide of World War II in their favor. When Japan's military leaders saw that their country was losing, they Scotch-taped flimsy little planes together and put bombs on the planes' noses. Then young pilots called kamikazes took off without enough fuel to return. Their goal was a suicidal mission—to crash into Allied ships, destroying both themselves and everyone on the vessels. They gave their lives in allegiance to the emperor, who was considered divine.

Paul was as radical as that, but for a different cause: to spread the gospel.

Today, a lot of Christians claim to be burned out. A pastor recently told me that he had asked a man in his church to lead worship. But the man begged off, saying, "I just can't take the strain of being a worship leader." The pastor wasn't asking him to work full-time. He just wanted him to lead people into worshiping Jesus with a few songs on Sundays. But it was too much.

Yet Paul, going through all kinds of suffering, never once used the word *burnout*. What was his secret?

Paul tapped into a resource that many of us today are missing. After writing about all his struggles, he said, "Though our bodies are dying, *our spirits are being renewed every day*" (2 Corinthians 4:16). Every day Paul found a way to get his inner person renewed.

We never eat breakfast and then say, "What a great meal! I don't need to eat for a week." Neither can we hear a great sermon and have its inspiration last for months. The inner person has to be renewed by God every day. When our inner persons are strong, we can deal with perplexities, challenges, difficulties, and persecutions and not give up. We remain, as Paul wrote in Ephesians 6:10, "strong in the Lord and in his mighty power."

Being renewed every day gave Paul an eternal perspective: "So we don't look at the troubles we can see now; rather, we fix our gaze on things that cannot be seen" (2 Corinthians 4:18). When we as Christians meet with Jesus every day through the Word and prayer, the invisible world will become real to us. The physical world—material things, our jobs, bills, selling a house—will no longer overwhelm us. Rather, we will be strengthened to live for what really matters.

"The things we see now," Paul wrote, "will soon be gone, but the things we cannot see will last forever" (2 Corinthians 4:18). Let's open our hearts today and let God renew our inner persons.

God, I know it's not your will for me to be overwhelmed. Renew me daily so that eternity becomes real to me and I can say, like Paul, "I never give up."

68

AN UNUSUAL WARNING

Stay away from people like that!

2 TIMOTHY 3:5

In 2 Timothy 3:5, the apostle Paul said a strange thing: "Avoid certain people." Christians have been commissioned by the Lord to win others to Christ, yet Paul was warning Timothy to stay away from certain people. Who would these people be?

Paul's warning began, through the inspiration of the Holy Spirit, with the statement that "in the last days there will be difficult times" (2 Timothy 3:1). That isn't the kind of positive pep talk most people want to hear. But Paul wasn't interested in tickling people's ears or entertaining them. He was determined to proclaim the truth of God, no matter the consequences.

In fact, there are no promises in the Bible that things are going to get better on planet Earth as the end draws near. Instead, many Scriptures say that things are going to get worse before Christ returns. We might not like that idea. But resisting it is like saying, "I don't like gravity. I want to jump off a building and fly like Superman," or "I want to eat junk food and see my cholesterol come down." Things don't work that way. None of us can do anything to alter the truth of God.

As Paul described the difficult days to come, he explained, "People will love only themselves and their money. They will be boastful and proud, . . . puffed up with pride, and love pleasure rather than God" (2 Timothy 3:2-4).

First, "people will love only themselves." Self will be their idol. They'll want what they want, when they want it, how they want it. They'll do anything to make more money and not think much about giving to the Lord. They'll also be "boastful and proud"—not humble, like lowly Jesus, the Son of God. And they'll "love pleasure rather than God." Whatever makes people feel good—every kind of entertainment—that's what they're going to be engrossed in.

All this is bad enough. But what Paul wrote next is what will make those times so terrible: "They will act religious, but they will reject the power that could make them godly" (2 Timothy 3:5). These people will be religious folk. They will attend church. They'll have Bibles. But as the Weymouth New Testament translates it, they will "keep up a make-believe of piety and yet live in defiance of its power." These people wouldn't *think* of missing a Sunday at church. But they will want the service to be short so they can get to what they really care about—themselves, money, and pleasure. Paul warned us to avoid people like that.

Let's examine ourselves, as 2 Corinthians 13:5 says we should, and make sure that we have a true relationship and fellowship with the risen Christ. He should be our number one desire. Being with him in heaven should be our great hope.

This warning to Timothy was not just for his life and times. Even more now, as difficult times are coming, we need to avoid the temptation to serve ourselves. Let's draw close to Jesus. He loves us more than anything we can imagine. When we draw near to him, as James 4:8 says, he will draw near to us.

Lord, thank you for warnings! Prepare me for the difficult days ahead. I want you to always have first place in my heart.

69

REMEMBER THE REMINDERS

I will always remind you about these things—
even though you already know them.

2 PETER 1:12

When I was growing up, my mom and dad were constantly giving me reminders. "Remember to clean the stairway," I was told. We lived in a three-story brownstone, and I had to sweep all the dirt and soot off the steps. After dinner, my mother would say, "Jim, it's your day to do the dishes. Your sister did them yesterday." I had been told these things already, but my parents felt that I needed reminders (which I did, because I wanted to get out of doing both those chores).

All of us, even when we have taken in a lot of God's Word, need spiritual reminders. Why? Because the truth is something we easily forget as a living reality. That's why there is so much repetition in the Scriptures—lots of reminders for our good.

How many times does the psalmist say, "It is good to praise the Lord," or "Sing to the Lord, all you people," or "Praise the Lord, for God is worthy of praise"? Or how many times did John, Paul, Peter, and Jesus himself tell us, "Love one another" (1 John 2:7); "Let love be your highest goal!" (1 Corinthians 14:1); "Show sincere love to each other" (1 Peter 1:22); "I am giving you a new commandment: Love each other" (John 13:34)?

"Why so much repetition?" we might ask. "We've got it."

No. God knows we need reminders, because the world around us has many voices calling us away from spiritual truth. Our hearts easily stray from the things that are most important to our lives and future destinies.

Peter didn't write his letter to give his readers numerous new revelations. When we are constantly looking for a new "revelation," we can easily end up in fanaticism. That's why Paul said in 1 Corinthians 4:6, "Do not go beyond what is written" (NIV). But what is written, we easily forget. That's why reminders are so important.

For example, we need to be reminded that Jesus is coming again. How many times have we all heard that? But do we live every day with the conscious thought, *This could be the day Jesus returns*? We need to be reminded of eternity, which will draw an end to life here on earth and be the start of our eternal home. If we keep that in mind, we will be diligent to do the work of God and win souls for Christ.

So as we read the Bible, we shouldn't skip over things we think we already know. Let's read slowly, even the verses we've seen many times, like Hebrews 11:6: "It is impossible to please God without faith." This Scripture reminds us that, more than anything, God wants us to trust him today. When we walk by faith, it makes God happy. We can cry a river, we can try to live better lives, we can make some big sacrifice, but without faith, it's impossible to please God. We need to hear that often.

Let's remember the reminders. Let's treasure them. God is repeating himself for a good reason. He loves us and wants to keep us close to him.

Lord, it's easy to read quickly over the parts in your Word that I'm familiar with. But help me to slow down! I want to take into my heart the rich reminders you have for me.

70

MORE IS SOMETIMES LESS

The LORD is able to give you much more than this!

2 CHRONICLES 25:9

When King Amaziah began ruling over Judah, one of his early tasks was to organize the army. He found that he had "300,000 select troops" who were "all trained in the use of spear and shield" (2 Chronicles 25:5). But the king wanted more soldiers. So he "also paid about 7,500 pounds of silver to hire 100,000 experienced fighting men from Israel" (2 Chronicles 25:6). Three hundred thousand is good, but four hundred thousand is better, right?

Not so fast. God has a different math.

The problem was that Israel, the northern kingdom, was filled with idol worshipers. So a man of God came to the king and said, "Your Majesty, do not hire troops from Israel, for *the Lord is not with Israel*" (2 Chronicles 25:7).

God is not with every person, or even every church, in the sense of blessing them and being pleased with them. The prophet was saying, "It's not how many men you have. The key thing is, *is God with you*? Because if you go into partnership with that bunch of idolaters, you're going to lose God's favor."

Now King Amaziah had paid a lot of silver for those extra troops from Israel. So he said to the prophet, "But what about all the money I spent? I'm going to lose 7,500 pounds of silver! They have a no-refund policy."

But the man of God replied, "The LORD is able to give you much more than this!" (2 Chronicles 25:9).

So Amaziah sent the hired troops back to Israel (see 2 Chronicles 25:10). He was about to fight the Edomites, so "Amaziah summoned his courage" (2 Chronicles 25:11) and led his army into battle. And God gave them victory.

Let's remember, we never lose by following God.

"I know," someone might say, "but he lost all that silver."

No, he didn't lose. He lost the money, but he had God with him. God did much more for Amaziah than 7,500 pounds of silver or those extra troops ever could have done.

How many times have I counseled people who wanted to compromise, especially when it comes to an event like a wedding? Instead of following their own convictions and honoring Christ, they say their Uncle Tony won't come unless they have hard liquor and a DJ who will play music with filthy lyrics and innuendos. "That's what they like, Pastor!"

"I know, but it's *your* wedding," I tell them. "Do you want to honor Christ, or do you want to please your family?"

"But if I honor Christ," they say, "I might lose out on those cash gifts. I need the money!"

Sometimes obeying God looks like a losing proposition. But any sacrifice, any holding to our convictions, any obedience to God will never end up hurting us. It will just bless us more. As the writer of Hebrews said, "Do not throw away this confident trust in the Lord. Remember the great reward it brings you!" (Hebrews 10:35). Today let's stick to what God told us to do. He will always give us a greater blessing than anything we could lose.

Lord, help me not to be afraid to lose material things or friends by obeying you. Thank you that when you are with me, I will never lose.

71

WHAT GOD LOOKS LIKE

Jesus replied, . . . "Anyone who has seen me has seen the Father!"

JOHN 14:9

God is a spirit, and no one has ever seen him in all his awesome splendor. But God loves us so much that he wants us to know what he's really like. That's one of the reasons he sent his Son, Jesus, to earth. Colossians 1:15 tells us that "Christ is the visible image of the invisible God." Jesus shows us exactly what God is like.

Some religious people, using isolated Scriptures, have created the image of a hideous God. But as I once heard someone say, "Any image of God outside the face of Jesus Christ is of the devil."

Yes, God gave us verses of Scripture describing himself. But the best way to know God is by studying the person of Jesus Christ. If we want to know how God feels about women, or children, or people who lose their way like lost sheep, we need to look at Jesus.

What do we learn about God in broad strokes by looking at the Lord?

We recognize that God loves us. No matter where we've been, what race we are, how old we are, or how many times we've messed up, God loves us. We know this because Jesus never walked by anyone and rejected them. He touched lepers. He restored people who had wrecked their lives. He freed demon-possessed people. He even kept loving his disciples, who failed and denied him.

Second, we learn that God hates sin. We see this in the way Jesus loved sinners but hated their sin. The Lord warned people about how a life of sin would hurt them, both here on earth and in the hereafter. My churchgoing dad took one drink at an office party and ended up an alcoholic for twenty-two years. He lost his job. He didn't attend my wedding. God hated what my dad's drunkenness did to my mother and our family, because it ended up hurting the people he loved. God hates sin.

That's why Jesus died on a cross. Sin is a very serious thing to God, no matter what the culture says. Sin is so horrible that there was no way God could cancel its penalty except by the sacrifice of his Son.

Finally, we realize God wants to bless us. Everywhere Jesus went, he did good and delivered those who were oppressed by the devil. Whenever we need help of any kind, we know God desires to come to our aid. We're sure of it, because Jesus is the exact image of the invisible God.

Satan will try to confuse us about what God is really like. When we have a good week, we think maybe he loves us. But when we fail to live up to our convictions, we suspect the Lord has turned his back on us. The truth is, God never changes. He loves us. He wants to save us from sin. He wants to bless us.

How do we know what God is like? Not by using a verse here and a verse there. We know what God is like by looking at Jesus.

Thank you, Lord, for sending your Son to earth so we could see what you are like. Help me see you as you are—by looking at Jesus.

72

NEVER ALONE

I am with you always.

MATTHEW 28:20

In both the Old and New Testaments, God promised, "I am with you" (Isaiah 41:10; Matthew 28:20). He said it over and over in different ways: "You don't have to be afraid" (see Isaiah 35:4; Matthew 10:31). "I'll go before you and behind you" (see Psalm 139:5). "I'll protect you from your enemies" (see Psalm 18:17). "You'll never be alone. Never" (see Deuteronomy 31:8; Hebrews 13:5).

Yet Christians often feel lonely. Christians get depressed. Believers can live in fear that some dark power from Satan is going to overwhelm them. They often don't live with a happy confidence that what God says is true. They read God's Word; they can repeat it verbally. Yet they still feel alone. In fact, the great plague in contemporary society is loneliness, and it often invades the lives of born-again believers in Jesus.

Why is that? Because only the Holy Spirit can make the promise "I am with you always" become a reality to us.

Having this statement from God in our heads is not enough. We need to spend time with the Lord and invite the Holy Spirit to come and make that promise—and many others—real to our souls. Having truth from the Bible in our heads is a good start. But Jesus promised that the Holy Spirit would reveal his teaching to our inner persons: "When the Father sends the Advocate as my representative—that is, the Holy Spirit—he will teach you everything and will remind you of everything I told you" (John 14:26).

When the Spirit teaches us, he doesn't speak only to our minds. He teaches the Word by revelation to our hearts. Then it becomes a reality to our souls and not just a mental construct. Without this revelation, or illumination, from the Holy Spirit, we will have head knowledge of God but not heart experience with the Lord.

We have all struggled at times to get hold of certain promises of God. We know that they are in the Bible, yet we can quote "My God will supply all your needs" (see Philippians 4:19) repeatedly and still go right back to being anxious about something we need. For me personally, only when I've taken the time to meditate on God's promises and wait on the Lord have I been able to say with the certainty of faith, "My God will supply all my needs."

When we fill ourselves with the Word of God and then let the Holy Spirit activate it in our hearts, faith and hope and confidence spring up everywhere. Instead of struggling to believe what God has declared is true, we find comfort and assurance rising in our hearts.

Let's ask God to make his unshakable promises real to us today. Then we will know with certainty, "God is with me. I am never alone."

Holy Spirit, come and make the promises of God real to my heart today. Let the truth that you are always with me, and all your other promises, come alive within me.

73

LEARNING TO LISTEN

Anyone with ears to hear should listen and understand!

MATTHEW 11:15

The brightest people in the world are often terrific listeners. That's one of the ways they've learned so much. People whose mouths are constantly moving, however, can't learn much because they're always expressing what they already know—or think they know.

This has much greater importance when it comes to God, who tells us not only to study his Word but also to listen to the voice of his Spirit. What we need today is for God to help us listen for and discern the quiet and often unusual ways he speaks.

When the prophet Elijah got discouraged, he ended up in a cave praying for help from God. And what happened next? First came a terrible windstorm, then an earthquake, and after that a blazing fire. But God wasn't in any of those. Then there came a gentle whisper, and that was how God revealed himself (see 1 Kings 19:9-13).

God doesn't always speak through thunder and lightning and powerful manifestations of the Spirit. Of course, he can communicate any way he sees fit. Sometimes he speaks through other people, or circumstances, or "accidents" of Providence. But many times he speaks with a still, small whisper in our hearts, and we have to learn to discern his voice. I'm not talking about so-called extrabiblical revelation and new doctrines. I'm talking about God guiding us in our decisions, showing us how to react to people, or giving us the solution to a problem within the framework of his Word.

A couple visiting our church recently approached me after a Sunday service. The man introduced the lady with him as his "partner in life." "I'm a Christian," he said. "I go to church regularly. I so enjoyed the meeting."

But I felt the Lord whisper to my heart, "There's a problem here." So I ventured out by faith, in love, saying, "You said this is your partner in life. Is this your wife?"

"Well, no."

Tenderly, I said, "I love you, brother. Are you living with her?"

He put his head down. "Yes."

I said, "Well, this is problematic. This is hurtful to God and to you. You say that you're a Christian, but you're living in sin that Jesus suffered and died on the cross for."

At that point the man led me away from the woman. He told me quietly that he had been previously married and divorced. "Pastor Jim," he said, "do you understand what divorce lawyers cost? I've worked hard and saved my money, and if I marry this woman and it goes south, I'll be left with nothing."

I said, "Well, then, leave her alone."

"No, I can't do that either."

So I said to him, "Well, look in my eyes, John. You're going to spend eternity in hell if you don't change the situation, because 1 Corinthians 6:9-10 says that anyone who willfully practices these things will never inherit the Kingdom of Heaven."

I knew it was the whisper of the Lord prompting me to help this man. I don't say to strangers, "Is that your wife?"

God loves us so much. He wants to speak direction, warnings, encouragement, and other guidance to our hearts. That's why Jesus taught us, "Anyone with ears to hear should listen and understand!" (Matthew 11:15). Let's ask the Lord today, "God, teach me to listen."

Lord, give me ears to hear the gentle, quiet voice of your Holy Spirit. I don't want to miss anything you have for me.

74

UNFINISHED BUSINESS

See to it that you complete the ministry you have received in the Lord.

COLOSSIANS 4:17, NIV

Imagine the drama. Paul had written a letter to the church in Colossae. He had never been to this church, but he kept track of the congregation there, and he loved the people. And now one of the leaders was reading his letter publicly. It had all kinds of doctrines about Christ, along with more practical matters pertaining to the believers' daily lives. Then, as Paul's closing statements were being read, out of nowhere one of the people in the church was named, right out in front of everyone: "Tell Archippus: 'See to it that you complete the ministry you have received in the Lord'" (Colossians 4:17, NIV).

Archippus was not an apostle or a preacher. He's mentioned only one other time in the Bible, in Philemon 1:2. But Paul, out of love for this man, said, "Complete the ministry you have received in the Lord." He was reminding Archippus, publicly, "God has given you a job to do—whether it's singing in the choir, working with children, serving in missions, being a prayer warrior, assisting the leadership, doing administration, encouraging others. See to it, Archippus, that you don't forget your calling." In fact, every one of us has a task the Lord has set before us.

But notice what's implied in Paul's reminder: Archippus had already begun the ministry. He had gotten grace and direction from

God and started doing what God had called him to do. But now Paul was saying, "Complete the ministry, Archippus. Don't stop halfway! You started it, and God is with you, so complete it."

I wonder how many of us have some unfinished business when it comes to our Christian lives. At some special moment, God called us to do something, and we stepped out and started it. And then, for some reason, we stopped.

Maybe Archippus got discouraged. Somebody criticized his work, and he said, "Why am I wasting my time with this? Well, I tried to do something. But then I heard 'He said,' 'She said,' 'They said.'" When any of us feels this way, that's the enemy working to discourage us.

Discouragement is not the only thing that causes us to quit. Sometimes we just get distracted from the task God gave us. We become so consumed with other things happening around us that we forget the calling of God, which has eternal reward written all over it.

Or we get tired. The calling of God involves *work*—not just physical work but also spiritual work against the opposition of Satan. The devil won't bother people too much who are consumed with the things of this world. But people who say, "No, I'm going to use my life for the building up of God's Kingdom and fulfill my calling," become targets of relentless satanic attacks because they are threats to the devil's kingdom. This often results in spiritual fatigue.

The real essence of spiritual warfare is staying with it when God has called us to something. Satan wants to stop us from completing the ministry the Lord has given us to do. But today we're going to arise and do it. God was with Archippus, and he's with us too. He will help us finish the work that we began.

Lord, what a privilege that you would call me to serve you. By your grace, let no discouragement, distraction, or tiredness keep me from finishing the task you've given me to do.

75

HEAVENLY REWARD

The wicked . . . look to this world for their reward.

PSALM 17:13-14

David, under the inspiration of the Holy Spirit, asked God to save him from the wicked. They wanted to attack him, surround him, throw him down (see Psalm 17:9-12).

But notice this: These people were not human traffickers. They were not embezzling money. They were not cursing God, as far as we know. What made them ungodly is that all their goals were in this physical world. "Rescue me, Lord," the psalmist prayed, "from those who look to this world for their reward!" (see Psalm 17:14).

Is this not a picture of the culture today? People are running after money, pleasure, or fame. They don't see the value of the invisible world—of God, his Spirit, sacrifice, soul-winning. Everything they're looking for is in the confines of the physical world.

The last thing Jesus said to his disciples before he went to heaven was, "Go into all the world and preach the gospel" (see Matthew 28:19). The whole thought was of sacrificing, going, boldly sharing the good news of Jesus. But I have heard denominational leaders say that the number of people volunteering for missions or training for ministry today is at an all-time low.

In years gone by, people of all ages have met God at some critical moment, knelt humbly in prayer, and seen the spiritual value of giving their lives to Christ for service. But many Christian colleges today don't have enough students who want to prepare themselves for a life of service. As a result, many former Bible schools and seminaries have been turned into full-fledged liberal arts universities. This keeps the schools open but very likely departs from the very reason they were founded.

Why is this trend so powerful? Because folks are seeking their reward in this world, not the other.

Recently our church honored an eighty-year-old Haitian woman named Elsie. Decades ago, I baptized her at a Tuesday night prayer meeting. When she got saved, she had a job in international banking and a nice apartment near the UN building. She prayed, "Lord, I'll go wherever you want me to go. Just don't send me back to Haiti."

Wouldn't you know it, God called her to Haiti to work among the poorest of the poor. She lived near a place in Port-au-Prince called the Ravines, a shantytown beyond description—no bathrooms, no lights at night. Elsie gave up everything to spend forty-plus years feeding children and sharing the gospel. When gangs took over Haiti and all hell broke loose, she stayed. She was in danger, but she still kept doing God's work.

Elsie looks to me as her pastor. But she doesn't know that Carol and I admire her more than she respects us. People might say, "Oh, that's nice. But she wasted her life." She didn't. And we should pity those who think that way. Their only reward is in this life. But, oh, the riches Elsie has waiting for her! I've told her, "I hope Carol and I live near you in heaven, because you're going to be in one of the best neighborhoods."

The question for us today is, are we living for this world and its rewards or for an eternal place where Christ dwells? Maybe we need to pray today, "Lord, get my eyes on heaven, eternity, and the value of serving others." Let's *live* in this life, but let's live for *Christ*.

Lord, help me see the emptiness of this world's rewards. I give my life to serve you. The reward in the next world will be worth it all.

76

TREASURING GOD'S WORD

The commandments of the Lord are right,
bringing joy to the heart.

PSALM 19:8

The main reason I wrote this devotional is to draw people to the Word of God. Spending time with Jesus is not about reading the one verse I chose and my little contribution about it. We must all walk by faith, and faith comes "by hearing, and hearing by the word of God" (Romans 10:17, KJV).

Satan wants to hinder us from experiencing a lot of things—prayer, church unity, the power of the Holy Spirit. But he absolutely wants to block us from reading God's Word, because without the Word, we won't have the faith required to live victoriously for Jesus. So he'll attack us by telling us that God's Word isn't real, that it's full of errors. Or he'll distract us, luring us toward other things to occupy our time and keep us away from the Bible.

In Psalm 19, David wrote about the many benefits of God's Word.

First, the Word of God revives the inner person (see Psalm 19:7). How many times have I been discouraged, too dead in my soul even to pray, but when I've gotten alone with God and opened that Bible and meditated on it, my soul has been revived. God's Word gives us spiritual get-up-and-go.

The Bible also gives us wisdom (see Psalm 19:7). We'll make better decisions for today—which is the only day we have—if we start out by filling ourselves with the Word of God.

The Word of God brings joy (see Psalm 19:8). We can come to the Word of God depressed, but when we read about God's love and faithfulness and his promises to never leave us, our sadness is replaced by joy.

God's Word also provides insight (see Psalm 19:8). As we deal with difficult situations or confusing circumstances, the Word of God gives us understanding.

The Bible gives us warnings as well (see Psalm 19:11). When we face temptations or the strategies of Satan, the Lord reminds us, "Remember what you read in my Word: 'There is a path before each person that seems right, but it ends in death'" (see Proverbs 14:12).

When the Word of God gets into our hearts—not just from reading it but as the Holy Spirit makes it alive to us—it also gives us new desires. The Word living in us will grant us victory over sin and Satan. It will give us a new desire to be kind to others and imitate Christ. It will create in us a desire to pray, because it shows us that prayer is not a waste of time. And it will give us a new way of looking at people, causing us to see them as souls made in the image of God instead of just a guy working behind a fast-food counter or a homeless person on the street.

Let's not quickly read a devotional book to get through it. Remember, the main thing that ruins all devotional time is the spirit of hurry. When we're rushing to the next thing and don't give the Spirit ample time, we miss much of the Word's power for our lives. Let's take time to be with Jesus every day in his Word—and see how it changes us gradually into the people God planned for us to be.

God, teach me to slow down and get your Word into my heart. Renew me, Lord, and give me new desires that will change the way I live.

77

MAKING GOD HAPPY

Do not bring sorrow to God's Holy Spirit.

EPHESIANS 4:30

The Holy Spirit is not a force or a power. He is a person. And like all of us, the Spirit can be made sad, and he can be made happy.

When we become born again, we are new creations, and the Holy Spirit comes to live within us. So when we sin—when we yield to temptation and fail God by action, word, or thought—we grieve, or sadden, the Spirit, who is holy.

A Christian admitted to me that when he had done something wrong one day, he could hardly sleep that night because the Holy Spirit had been so grieved and had convicted his heart. The man lost his sense of peace and joy. Why? Because when we grieve the Spirit, we lose the beautiful benefits he was sent to produce in us.

One of the reasons many of us hurt the Holy Spirit is because we tend to be people pleasers. The Old Testament prophets faced this, especially Jeremiah. He lamented, pouring out his heart to God, "Lord, you send me to the people with messages they don't want to hear. They even mock me and want to kill me. Yet if I don't say what you tell me, I'll grieve you" (see Jeremiah 20:7-9). Many of us have felt pressured to go against God to please people. But as I once heard someone say, "It's better to make everyone in the world sad than to grieve God."

Years ago, when I left my job in the business world to go into the ministry, my mom was not thrilled with my decision. She was married to an alcoholic, and she had been beaten down by life. She also was worried about financial resources for my family. In order to make my mother happy, I would have had to say no to God's calling on my life. It hurt me to hurt my mother, but I had to please the Lord.

Sometimes unbelieving friends want us to join in their partying and lifestyle choices. But it's better to let them down and be at peace with our consciences and the Holy Spirit.

People have come to me over the years and said, "You know, we love your wife's music, and your preaching is okay. But your meetings are so long. We're used to, like, fifty-five minutes to an hour ten. I mean, we tithe here regularly, so can't you shorten the thing?" Should I please those people and covet their tithes? Or should I try, under God, to make the Spirit happy by following his leading?

If we want to follow the command of Ephesians 6:10 and "be strong in the Lord and in his mighty power"—i.e., the power of the Spirit—then we can't regularly cause him anguish. May God help us today to be sensitive to the mind and heart of the Holy Spirit. Let's ask God for grace to please him, no matter what others think or feel, so that we can have his smile upon us.

God, give me grace and wisdom to walk in such a way that I don't make the Holy Spirit sad. Even when others don't understand my actions, I want to please you above all else.

78

UNLIKELY PEOPLE

Elizabeth was unable to conceive, and they were both very old.

LUKE 1:7

God foretold, through many Old Testament prophets, that the Messiah would one day come. All those prophecies were fulfilled through the birth of Jesus. But in Malachi 3:1, we find a prophecy about somebody God would send before the Messiah, who would prepare the way for him. This was John the Baptist, of whom Jesus said, "Of all who have ever lived, none is greater" (Matthew 11:11).

If we were God and could pick the parents to raise the forerunner of the Messiah, whom would we choose? We would definitely pick a couple in their mid-twenties, perfect for childbearing. We'd probably choose upper middle class people so the child could be trained in the best schools and have an influential rabbi pour knowledge into him as he grew up.

Yet whom did the Lord pick to be the parents of John the Baptist? An elderly priest, Zechariah, and his barren wife, Elizabeth.

Notice why: "Zechariah and Elizabeth were righteous in God's eyes, careful to obey all of the Lord's commandments and regulations" (Luke 1:6). God doesn't prioritize intelligence or wealth. Instead, he delights in integrity and godliness. Still, why would he purposely choose an old man married to a barren woman (see Luke 1:7)? It was an impossible situation.

Even Zechariah was shocked when the angel Gabriel announced to him, "Your wife will give birth to the forerunner of the Messiah."

Zechariah's response wasn't surprising: "Are you sure? I mean, is this for real?" (see Luke 1:11-18).

So what can we learn from this story?

First, God loves to choose unlikely people and circumstances to do wonderful things so that his name will be glorified. Maybe you feel like an unlikely person today, but you have a desire to live for the Lord and be used by him. You may think you're not qualified, but you are. You're not too old, too young, or too uneducated. God is not looking for our ability, but rather our availability. He loves to take impossible situations and show that with him, nothing is impossible.

Second, when the angel appeared to Zechariah, he gave that beautiful word, "Don't be afraid, Zechariah! God has heard your prayer" (Luke 1:13). Zechariah and Elizabeth had prayed and prayed, probably for years, to have a child. Now in their senior years, they likely had given up asking. But God had heard and stored away their prayers. They were an unlikely couple, without much that the world would value. But they believed in God and prayed. That would be the best environment for baby John to grow up in.

The Bible is full of stories with unlikely scenarios. God waited until Abraham was too old and then gave him a child, saying, "Your descendants will be more than the stars in the sky" (see Genesis 15:5). He directed Samuel to pick David, the youngest of Jesse's sons, who said to Jesse, "That's the one who will be king" (see 1 Samuel 16:12).

Let's be encouraged today. No matter how hopeless things might seem, we have a God whose ways are not our ways and whose thoughts are not our thoughts (see Isaiah 55:8). As we walk in faith, close to the Lord, he will take our impossibilities and use them for his glory.

Oh, Lord, sometimes I feel like an unlikely person. But with you all things are possible! Even when I can't see how you will work things out, I will trust you.

79

SAFE UNDER THE BLOOD

When I see the blood, I will pass over you.

EXODUS 12:13

On the night he delivered Israel from four hundred years of slavery, God severely judged Egypt. Pharaoh had refused to let the people go, even after God had released nine plagues on the nation. So the tenth and final plague would be a night of judgment on all the gods of Egypt and the people who worshiped them.

As the time approached, God told Moses to have each Hebrew family choose a lamb. Then, at twilight on the fourteenth of the month, every family was to kill its lamb and smear some of its blood on the doorframes of their houses. This was the start of Passover, which is celebrated to this day as an annual Jewish high holy day. It was also the forerunner of the Lord's Supper, or Communion. That's why Jesus, the Lamb of God who would shed his blood for us, said, "Do this in remembrance of me" (see 1 Corinthians 11:23-26).

After slaughtering the lambs, the Israelites were commanded to stay in their houses. "No one," God said, "may go out through the door until morning" (Exodus 12:22). Why? Because God was going to send the death angel to kill the firstborn son of every Egyptian. The Lord was reminding the Hebrews, "Even though you're children of Abraham, Isaac, and Jacob, if you go outside, you'll meet the same judgment as the Egyptians."

This is a picture of the future final judgment upon the earth and its inhabitants. God was only judging Egypt then. But the universal promise of God stands true: "Each person is destined to die once and after that comes judgment" (Hebrews 9:27).

Note the most critical part of what God said in Exodus 12:13: "When I see the blood, I will pass over you." Not "When *you* see the blood." Not "When you *understand* the blood." No. The Lord said, "When *I* see the blood, I will pass over you."

But what if some of those Israelites were not acting the way they should? Maybe a husband and wife had argued that very day. It didn't matter. The judgment was made on this basis: If God saw the blood, they received mercy. If there was no blood, they were doomed.

Now if God seeing the blood of an innocent animal saved the Israelites on Passover night, how must the Lord treasure and value the blood of his own Son, Jesus? We who have accepted Christ as our Savior by putting, as it were, his blood on the doorposts of our hearts will be saved by that once-for-all sacrifice of Jesus.

So if Satan accuses us today, saying, "You did this ten years ago, ten days ago, ten minutes ago. You're no Christian. God has it in for you," the only way to overcome him is by the blood of the Lamb. "Say whatever you want, Satan," we can reply. "I am safe under the blood of Jesus. If you have an argument against me, go talk to him. Jesus told me to trust in what he did on the cross, and I have."

"If the Son sets you free, you are truly free" (John 8:36). Let's not live in guilt or condemnation today. Let's live in the freedom of the children of God, who have been washed in the blood.

Thank you, Jesus, for your blood that covers me.
What a comfort that I am free from judgment
when I rest in what you have done for me.

80

DON'T FORGET!

How quickly they forgot what he had done!

PSALM 106:13

Psalm 106 starts out on a joyful note: "Praise the Lord! Give thanks to the Lord, for he is good! His faithful love endures forever." The psalmist was practically bursting with praise. "Who can list the glorious miracles of the Lord? Who can ever praise him enough?" (Psalm 106:1-2).

But then things took a turn. "Our ancestors in Egypt were not impressed by the Lord's miraculous deeds. They soon forgot his many acts of kindness to them" (Psalm 106:7), including his miraculous deliverance of them from Egypt. Instead, they rebelled by the Red Sea when they saw Pharaoh's army closing in on them. "Why did you bring us out here to die in the wilderness?" (Exodus 14:11), they cried to Moses.

Yet God still saved them, leading them through the sea on dry land. When they saw the chariots of Egypt overcome by the rushing waters that God had divided for them, "then his people believed his promises. Then they sang his praise" (Psalm 106:12). Surely now they would mature and go from faith to faith and glory to glory!

Unfortunately, they didn't. Psalm 106:13 says, "Yet how quickly they forgot what he had done!" They began complaining about shortages of food and water. They grew envious of Moses. They even built a golden calf and worshiped it! Instead of going from glory to glory and grace to grace, the Israelites went from disgrace to more disgrace and from disobedience to worse disobedience.

The psalmist put his finger on the problem: "How quickly they forgot!"

I've been guilty of that. How about you? God has had to remind me, "After all I've done for you and your wife and the church you pastor, how can you complain and not believe? Look back. Remember what I've already done."

The Bible says that there are certain things we're to forget. But there are also certain things that are vital to remember. Forgetting none of his benefits (see Psalm 103:2) will help us look back over our lives and rejoice in God's incredible faithfulness. Otherwise, we will be overwhelmed by our circumstances, and we'll forget God's track record. Then we'll most likely fail to trust the Lord for divine intervention.

What has God done for you in the last week, the last month, the last year? What has he done in your family, your finances, and, most of all, your spiritual growth? None of us is what we want to be, but if we're Christians, we're sure not what we used to be. Who made all those changes? Our faithful Father did.

We should never forget the Lord and his goodness to us. Instead, let's remember the words of a song I heard growing up: "When I think of the goodness of Jesus and what he has done for me, my soul cries out, 'Hallelujah!' Praise God for saving me."[14]

Today, let's sit down and close our eyes for a few minutes and allow God to direct our minds to all he's done for us, both the big and little things. In the face of adversity, we don't need to panic, like the Israelites did at the Red Sea, and say, "What are we going to do now?" God has proven over and over again that his Word is true: "I will never leave you or forsake you" (see Hebrews 13:5). Let's remember that promise today.

Lord, you have done so many things for me.
Thank you, God. I know that you will take
care of every problem facing me today.

81

THORNY GROUND

Other seed fell among thorns that grew up and choked out the tender plants.

MARK 4:7

Every Christian knows that God's Word is powerful, "sharper than the sharpest two-edged sword" (Hebrews 4:12). It's the seed that can bring forth "thirty, sixty, and even a hundred times" what was sown (Mark 4:8).

But in Jesus' parable of the sower recorded in the book of Mark, not every seed bore fruit. Some of the farmer's seeds fell among thorns. Beneath the soil, in the dark where no one could see, the seeds' outer hulls broke away, and the miracle of life began—not unlike the Word of God coming alive in people's hearts. Yet Jesus said that the thorns "grew up and choked out the tender plants so they produced no grain" (Mark 4:7). These new plants, full of beautiful potential, were stymied because of a foreign, aggressive growth in the soil alongside the seeds. It's a spiritual mystery how God's Word is all powerful, yet it came to nothing in the case of the ground littered with thorns.

When the disciples were alone with Jesus and asked him to explain the parable, he said, "The seed that fell among the thorns represents others who hear God's word, but all too quickly the message is crowded out by the worries of this life, the lure of wealth, and the desire for other things, so no fruit is produced" (Mark 4:18-19). That's a tragic ending, right?

It's not drug addiction or drunkenness or lying on our tax returns that chokes the Word. It's "the worries of this life." Instead of letting the Word of God work with divine power in us, the cares and worries connected to everyday life strangle the budding seed planted in us.

The "lure of wealth" can also choke God's Word in our lives. Money promises fulfillment, but it's a liar. Even when our wealth increases, we're not satisfied. We need more riches. And when we have more, then we need more and more.

Finally, "the desire for other things," or materialism, stifles the Word. We're not satisfied with what we already have. We've got to have the newest phone, newest car, newest sneakers, newest dress. These things seem innocuous, but according to Jesus, they can stymie the power of the Word of Almighty God!

I had a friend who once bought fifty pounds of walnuts. He didn't like walnuts, but he said he couldn't pass up the sale. Some people amass stuff they'll never use, like the lady politician from the Far East who had more than a thousand pairs of shoes.

The worries of life, the lure of wealth, and the desire for material things can choke the precious seed of God's Word. There's no other way to read this passage.

Instead of being suffocated by the things of this world, we can sing the chorus of this old hymn: "More, more about Jesus. More, more about Jesus. More of his saving fullness see, more of his love who died for me."[15] Let's not live for things that choke out God's Word in our hearts. Let's live for more of Jesus.

God, clear out the thorns in my heart. Deliver me from worry, which is a sin according to your Word. Deliver me from being greedy for money. And deliver me from covetousness, always wanting more.

82

THE BEST TEACHER

The Spirit teaches you everything you need to know.

1 JOHN 2:27

When I was called into the ministry, I immediately felt compelled to learn the Bible from cover to cover the best I could. So I started building a library. I collected commentaries and devotional books on a wide range of subjects. I bought different versions of the Bible. I started a Bible-reading plan, and every day I still read something from the Old Testament, the Psalms, and the New Testament.

But for many years, all I understood about the Bible was what someone else had written about it. I didn't realize that God had something better. Not that I needed to throw away my books. But I needed to learn to trust the Holy Spirit to be my personal teacher—to unveil to me, through revelation, the depths of his Word.

We all need this. We need God to open the eyes of our hearts so we can understand the Bible and apply it to our lives. Scripture is better taught by the Holy Spirit than by any human teacher.

The apostle John made that clear. "The Holy Spirit lives inside you," he wrote, "so you don't need anyone to teach you. The Spirit will teach you everything you need to know" (see 1 John 2:27).

If this is true, then why has God put pastors and teachers in the church (see Ephesians 4:11)? Well, there is a place for teachers. But teachers can't be with us every day. God wants to reveal things to us as we read his Word prayerfully, humbly, thoughtfully. After all, the Holy Spirit wrote the book. Who could better explain a book than the person who wrote it?

When the disciples were puzzled by something Jesus taught, they went to him. "Lord," they asked, "what did you mean when you said that?" But now Jesus is in heaven. Before he was taken up into the clouds, he said, "When I leave, I will send you another helper. I've been with you, but he will be *in* you. He will teach you everything" (see John 14:16-17, 26). How we need to ask the Holy Spirit, before we open our Bibles, "Lord, teach me. Open my eyes that I may see wonderful things in your law" (Psalm 119:18, NIV)!

There's a danger in venerating a spiritual teacher to the place that God has given the Holy Spirit. "Oh, I've got to ask the pastor what he thinks," some people say. That's okay. It's not a bad thing. And let's read what we can from men and women of God. But is there no living Holy Spirit anymore? He lives within us as Jesus' representative and wants to teach us the Word.

Now some people have abused this. They believe that God is always talking to them, and the things they think he's saying are sometimes contrary to the Bible. But when we see that, the danger is to react by saying, "We don't want that fanaticism. No, no, let's just use our good old-fashioned IQs." But our IQs are deficient.

The Holy Spirit is waiting to teach us today. He is in the classroom, but we're out in the hallway. Let's go in, take a seat, and say, "Spirit of the living God, teach me. You wrote the Bible. Now explain it to me."

Lord, with the psalmist I pray, open my eyes to the wonderful things in your Word. Give me something fresh from the Scriptures today.

83

INCONVENIENT ANCESTORS

David was the father of Solomon (whose mother was Bathsheba, the widow of Uriah).

MATTHEW 1:6

A friend of mine heard that one of his ancestors had fought in the Mexican-American War. So he dug into his family tree. He wanted to be able to say, "My ancestor was one of the illustrious people who fought at the Alamo." Well, it turned out that his great-great-ancestor had been at the Alamo—but he had deserted and been shot in the back by his commanding officer as he ran away. When he discovered that, my friend said he wanted to blow up his family tree.

Jesus, since he was all God yet all man, had both divine ancestry and human ancestry.

Now God could have picked any family line for Jesus' human ancestry. We might expect that God would have put some really eminent names in there. And some of the people in Jesus' lineage do have greatness associated with their names: Abraham, the father of faith. David, the great king. Solomon, the wisest king.

But in Matthew's genealogy of Jesus, we find something strange. As we're reading through the list of men, we suddenly come to "Salmon was the father of Boaz (whose mother was Rahab)" (Matthew 1:5). Why did Matthew mention a woman? On top of that, Rahab was a prostitute. Why note that unfortunate fact?

Later Matthew mentioned another woman: "David was the father of Solomon (whose mother was Bathsheba, the widow of Uriah)"

(Matthew 1:6). Why bring up the woman associated with the darkest episode in David's life?

We read in 2 Samuel 11 that when David should have been out leading the armies of Israel on the battlefield, he stayed at home. One night from his rooftop, he saw a beautiful woman bathing on another rooftop. He called for her, and a very bad one-night stand ensued.

When Bathsheba found out she was pregnant, David called her husband, Uriah, back from battle. Uriah was one of David's leading military men. David wanted him to go be with his wife so that it would look like the baby was Uriah's. But this man was so loyal to David that he wouldn't go home. He slept on the steps of the palace.

So David concocted an evil plan. He sent Uriah back to the battle with a note for the commander, Joab. It read, "Attack the city, and then have everybody withdraw but Uriah so he'll die." (Imagine putting that in writing! Talk about an email trail.) So Uriah was abandoned as ordered, and he died in battle. But really, David killed him.

So why mention Bathsheba in the genealogy?

Because God wanted us to know that the Messiah, who descended humanly from Abraham, Isaac, Jacob, David, and Solomon, came to earth for people who have wrecked their lives. God delights in showing mercy to people who are filled with shame, guilt, and condemnation. Judgment is his "strange act" (Isaiah 28:21, KJV). In other words, he doesn't like to punish us. No. The Lord loves taking people out of the mud and cleaning them off.

No wonder the baby in Bethlehem was to be named Jesus, for he would "save his people from their sins" (Matthew 1:21). Let's rejoice in what God has done for us. And let's carry that same spirit of mercy with us today, not looking down on anyone. There but for the grace of God go you and I.

Thank you, God, that you delight in showing mercy to sinners! Give me your heart for others who need your love today.

84

WHERE THE ACTION IS

Let us approach the throne of grace with boldness.

HEBREWS 4:16, CSB

In the late 1970s, the talk of the town in New York City was the infamous Studio 54. People were looking for the best disco, the most beautiful people, and plentiful drugs. Studio 54 had it all. It was the place to go for action of every kind.

The Christian life also has a place where the greatest things are going on. But we don't have to wait until the weekends. It's available to us all the time. The Bible is always, in one way or another, pointing us to this place. Hebrews 4:16, for example, tells us, "Let us approach the throne of grace." Where's the action? It's the place of prayer.

The writer of Hebrews pointed out that Jesus is greater than the angels, greater than Moses, greater than the Jewish high priest. But this "great High Priest" also "understands our weaknesses" (Hebrews 4:14-15). Jesus has tremendous sympathy and compassion for people who are in need. He is the great helper. But his help is administered at a special place: the throne of grace.

Notice, the author doesn't just tell us to come to the place of prayer. We are to come "with boldness." The word *boldness* brings to mind the idea of speaking freely, telling God the whole story without hedging, without embarrassment. We don't need to ask, "Am I good enough?" We don't need to look for the right moment, like when I was growing up and wanted to ask my mother for money. No, the Bible tells us, "Come boldly, no matter where you are, what you've done, or how you feel."

So what can we obtain at the throne of grace? We can find two beautiful things waiting for us there: "We will receive his mercy, and we will find grace" (Hebrews 4:16).

Why would Christians need mercy? We're already clean through the shedding of Jesus' blood on the cross, right? But believers fail the Lord every day in some way, shape, or form. So to keep our accounts straight with God, we come boldly but humbly to the throne of grace, and God will give us mercy.

We also get *grace* at the place of prayer. What is grace? The general definition is God's unmerited favor—God doing for us something that we don't deserve. We don't deserve forgiveness of sins and eternal life, but God gives them to us by grace. Another definition for grace that I've loved over the years is God doing for us what we can't do for ourselves. Grace could be the wisdom we need, strength for the day, or comfort when our hearts have been broken. It's God's love in action.

Also notice, grace comes just "when we need it most" (Hebrews 4:16). A well-known preacher from generations ago pointed out that the Greek phrase translated "in time of need" means "in the nick of time."[16] In other words, God's grace is there for us exactly when we need it.

Do you need mercy today? How about grace? I need them every day. Every hour. Every time a new situation arises that was unexpected. We must learn to go daily to the throne of grace, claiming the mercy and grace God has promised. And we've got to keep going again and again, because all we will ever need is waiting for us there.

Let's boldly approach the throne of grace today.

Lord, I need mercy for things I've done in the past. And I need grace to move forward today. Thank you, Lord, that I can come boldly to you.

85

MEASURING SPIRITUALITY

If you claim to be religious but don't control your tongue, you are fooling yourself.

JAMES 1:26

James, the half brother of our Lord, was a straight talker. His epistle didn't focus primarily on doctrinal truth but rather on practical daily living. For example, "It doesn't matter how religious you are. If your mouth runs wild, you're self-deceived" (see James 1:26). According to James, the tongue must be controlled or our religion is in vain.

When the doctor says, "Stick out your tongue," it's because the tongue is an indicator of what's going on in the body. It's the same spiritually. The tongue is a barometer of where we are with the Lord.

James wrote that we should "be quick to listen, slow to speak, and slow to get angry" (James 1:19). Yet too often we talk before we think, and our words can really leave some emotional scar tissue. I have counseled countless Christian couples who have said harsh things to each other in the heat of an argument, and years later the devil is still reminding them of those cutting remarks. "Remember how she said you're good for nothing?" or "You know, he said he was going to leave you." Words can be more painful than a punch in the stomach.

That's why the Bible teaches that the tongue must come under our control.

The trouble is, as James wrote, "we all make many mistakes. For if we could control our tongues, we would be perfect and could also control ourselves in every other way" (James 3:2). In other words, the sign of true maturity is controlling the tongue—but nobody can do it. Years ago, people trained lions and tigers for shows in Las Vegas. But the tongue? Forget it. It's uncontrollable.

Only God can do it.

When I was in college, I began seeking God. One Sunday night in a service, my heart was so hungry for the Lord. The Holy Spirit was moving, blessing, and breaking me. I went to the altar and poured out my heart to the Lord, and he filled me with a fresh river of grace. Oh, my heart was overflowing with God's love.

Afterward, I went to a house where a group of Christians were gathering for food and fellowship. My heart was still in tune with God; I couldn't stop worshiping him in my heart. But people started talking about others who weren't there, tearing into them, almost mocking them. I couldn't take it. The malicious words spoken around me were like daggers to my soul. I got up and headed alone to the living room, where I began to weep.

The same tongue we use to praise God one minute can spew ugly words about people the next. "Does a spring of water bubble out with both fresh water and bitter water?" James asked (James 3:11). No. Oh, the hurt we can cause with our tongues!

Why don't we ask God to help us today, by his Spirit, to control our tongues? His grace can teach us when to talk, when to be silent, what to say, and what not to say. He can guide us about which subjects to avoid. Then our words will be "good and helpful" and "an encouragement to those who hear them" (Ephesians 4:29). Let's not permit a loose tongue to make our religion be in vain.

God, help me. Make today a day of you controlling my tongue so that beautiful, healthy words that help others will come out of my mouth.

86

A MODEL CHURCH

You became a model to all the believers in Macedonia and Achaia.

1 THESSALONIANS 1:7, NIV

When Paul preached the good news of Jesus Christ to the people of Thessalonica, they "received the message with joy from the Holy Spirit" (1 Thessalonians 1:6). Hearing later of their vibrant faith, Paul wrote to them, "You have become an example to all the believers in Greece" (1 Thessalonians 1:7). The Holy Spirit, speaking through Paul, was holding up this church as a model.

Model churches today are usually measured by attendance, size of campus, and annual income. But this is not how Scripture evaluates things. So what did this model church in Thessalonica look like?

Number one, this church was known for its faith. "Wherever we go," Paul wrote, "we find people telling us about your faith in God" (1 Thessalonians 1:8). We don't know if the church had a hundred people or five hundred, but they had deep faith, and everyone knew that they were true believers. A church can have large attendance numbers, but if the people in the pews are not full of faith in Jesus Christ, it will not be pleasing to God (see Hebrews 11:6).

We are also told that the believers in this church had "turned away from idols to serve the living and true God" (1 Thessalonians 1:9). This was mostly a Gentile church, and the people had been steeped in idolatry. But these believers weren't just attending church on Sundays. They had stopped worshiping idols and begun serving the living God, who was now directing their lives. That's the kind of turnaround only Jesus can accomplish.

Finally, the Thessalonian believers were "looking forward to the coming of God's Son from heaven—Jesus, whom God raised from the dead. He is the one who has rescued us from the terrors of the coming judgment" (1 Thessalonians 1:10). These words are both an encouragement and a warning. As God's people, we are to wait for the return of Jesus Christ, which could happen at any moment of any day—even while you're reading this devotional.

A friend of mine, decades ago, was one of the most popular gospel songwriters in America. His publishing company made a lot of money from his creative talent. But when he wrote a musical about the return of Jesus Christ called *Behold, He Cometh*, the company executives told him, "We'll pass on that one. Nobody wants to hear that Jesus is coming back at any moment. They have plans to visit the Caribbean or Disney World. The Second Coming would ruin everything." The publishing company had its finger on the pulse of much of American Christianity. But a church that pleases God will be looking for the return of Jesus.

Notice, Jesus is coming to rescue us from the coming wrath. He's not coming to be born in a manger and rejected and crucified again. No, no, no. He's coming to judge the living and the dead on the "day of wrath" (Zephaniah 1:15, NIV). But those of us who have put our faith in Jesus will not see the wrath of God, because Jesus bore it on the cross for us.

Let's ask God today to make us like those Christians in Thessalonica—full of joyful faith, serving the living God, and looking forward to the return of the Lord Jesus Christ.

Thank you, Lord, for showing us your idea of a model church. Today, make us like the church in Thessalonica so that our faith will spread and you will be pleased.

87

BEARING FRUIT

Let our people learn to devote themselves to good works.

TITUS 3:14, CSB

The Lord taught the disciples, "If you abide in me, you will bear much fruit. This brings great glory to my Father" (see John 15:5-8). Paul wasn't there when Jesus taught that, but he came to understand it well. That's why he wrote to Titus, a spiritual son he had left on the island of Crete to be an overseer in the church, saying, "Let our people learn to devote themselves to good works for pressing needs, so that they will not be unfruitful" (Titus 3:14, CSB).

When Jesus said "abide" in me, he was saying, "Remain connected to me. Stay with me, and I will stay with you." As Christians, we are joined together with Christ—not with a church, not with Christian activity, but with Jesus—so we can bear fruit. And one way fruit can be seen is through good works.

God wants to give us the grace and discernment to let our light shine and do good deeds. We must not merely think about doing good works or feel pity on the less fortunate. We must actually do something to help others, by the grace of God working through us. As we do good deeds on a daily basis, we will not be unfruitful.

Here's a good question for all of us: Are we bearing fruit in our daily lives?

It's all too easy to have a kind of religious life that doesn't show itself in doing good to others. That's partially because good works have been underplayed in our day. Some Christians say, "Salvation is by grace through faith. Why do good works matter? I'm saved by what Jesus did on the cross." While that is all true, Jesus is our example, and he went about doing good. This is the kind of life that pleases our Father.

Some people just need a word of encouragement. Others can be taken out to lunch or prayed over or visited in the hospital.

When I was a college student with the spiritual depth of a fig, I was attending a church, but I was mostly just full of myself. Everything revolved around my life, my plans, my problems. But an associate pastor in the church took time with me. Every chance this man had, he and I went out for coffee, and he talked to me and listened to me. He directed my mind toward spiritual things and told me stories about God's dealings with him. What an effect that had on my life! I look at him now as one of the three or four most influential people in my life. He never became a famous Christian leader, but he did the good work of encouraging and showing kindness to a confused college student.

We can't do any good works last week. The past is gone. Tomorrow we might be able to do good works, if God grants it. But today the Lord will definitely give us opportunities—this very day that you're reading this devotion—to do good works. We can be kind to someone. We can offer words of encouragement. We can meet a need. When we do these things, we will prove to be fruitful, and that will glorify God.

God, help me stay close to you today so I can be fruitful. Help me notice others in their need and do good to them—so I can bring glory to you.

88

LEAVE IT WITH GOD

I leave it all in the L*ORD's hand;*
I will trust God for my reward.
ISAIAH 49:4

Any Christian who wants to do work for the Lord will sometimes feel down-and-out. We give ourselves to working with young people or sharing Christ with an unsaved friend, but we don't see obvious results. Then the enemy comes in and says, "What's the point? You're exerting energy, but nothing's happening."

The prophet Isaiah knew this feeling. The Lord had called him to the ministry and told him, "You are my servant. You will bring me glory" (see Isaiah 49:3). So Isaiah, like the Christians in Ephesus later, exhibited a life of "hard work" and "patient endurance" (Revelation 2:2). Yet after all he had done, the prophet cried to God, "But my work seems so useless! I have spent my strength for nothing and to no purpose" (Isaiah 49:4).

I've had many days in the ministry when I poured out my heart preaching, and the result was seemingly nothing. I didn't know if my sermons were that bad or if the people weren't listening, but I thought, *I really must be the worst preacher in America. What's the use?*

But Isaiah knew something that all of us need to understand: His feelings had nothing to do with the Lord's faithfulness. So after crying out to God, he said, "Yet I leave it all in the Lord's hand; I will trust God for my reward" (Isaiah 49:4).

We can sing in the choir, work with children, or minister to the homeless and see no discernable fruit from it, but our real reward doesn't come in the here and now. It will come from the Lord.

In the mid-1940s, one of the biggest ministries geared to teenagers was Youth for Christ.[17] They had a famous speaker named Torrey Johnson, and his office accidentally double-booked him for a certain date. So they had to tell one group, "Sorry, he can't come."

"But we're excited," they said. "He's got to come."

The scheduler in the Youth for Christ office offered a solution. "Listen," he said, "we've got this young evangelist who just started with us. His name is Billy Graham. We'll send him so you're not hung out to dry."

They responded, "We don't want Billy Graham. We want Torrey Johnson."

Young Billy Graham came, though, and he did his best to present the good news of Jesus Christ.

When he gave an invitation for people to receive Christ, only one person responded. Billy Graham went home thinking, *Maybe I'm not cut out for this.*

But guess who that one convert was? It was a young Warren Wiersbe, who later became pastor of Moody Church and a great Bible expositor who wrote hundreds of books. Warren Wiersbe blessed people around the world with his scriptural insights, to the point that a lot of preachers still use his sermon outlines. While Billy Graham was thinking, *What am I doing this for?* God was already preparing him to touch unimagined numbers of people in the future.

We don't know what God is doing behind the scenes when we give ourselves to his work. But like a song my wife wrote says, "Though we often don't know just how, God is working . . . even now."[18] Let's keep serving the Lord, even when it seems as if there are no results. One day, whether on earth or in heaven, we will see our reward.

Lord, let me be faithful to serve you today,
knowing that my reward is with you.

89

PRAYING IN THE SPIRIT

We do not know what to pray for as we should,
but the Spirit himself intercedes for us.
ROMANS 8:26, CSB

One of the richest chapters in the New Testament to me has always been Romans 8. In this chapter Paul focused on the life-giving Spirit of God, who sets us free from the law of sin and death.

The Holy Spirit does many beautiful things for us. He lets us know that we are God's children (see Romans 8:16). He also gives us "a foretaste of future glory," when we will be fully "released from sin and suffering" (Romans 8:23). But one of the other things the Spirit does for us is something we probably experience the least: "We do not know what to pray for as we should, but the Spirit himself intercedes for us with inexpressible groanings" (Romans 8:26, CSB). In other words, the Holy Spirit can teach us how to pray.

For those of us living in the Western world, even for many who have been raised in church, the idea of letting our minds be less active and opening ourselves to the influence of the Holy Spirit is foreign to us. We might identify it as emotionalism or fanaticism. But it's totally biblical. The Father is seeking those who will worship him "in Spirit and in truth" (John 4:23, CSB), and that applies to prayer, too.

This kind of prayer wasn't foreign to Paul. Notice his bold statement: "We do not know what to pray for as we should." Both in content and fervency, Paul realized our need of the Spirit in prayer. Sometimes what we pray for is relatively unimportant, and what we really need we don't even get to. We need the Spirit to give us intensity, faith, and direction so we can pray as we should.

Jude also told us to "pray in the power of the Holy Spirit" (Jude 1:20). Many Christians would say, "What does that mean? I ask God to watch over my kids at school, or to help me get that promotion." But the Holy Spirit wants to direct our spirits to the kind of prayer that is effectual and fervent and releases tremendous power as we lay our needs before God (see James 5:16).

The Spirit also helps us pray "with inexpressible groanings." Sometimes what we feel is so deep, so unspeakable, that the Holy Spirit helps us to express it with deep groans or even tears. The Spirit working with our inner person takes us into depths we could never go with our minds alone. With these deep longings or cries, sometimes we don't know exactly what we're praying for. But we don't have to understand it, because according to Romans 8:27, God understands what the prayer is about.

One day at the end of a church service when I invited people to come forward to pray, I saw a young Asian lady quietly weeping. When the song we were singing ended, I felt impressed to encourage her. So I said, in front of everyone, "Young lady, don't you be ashamed of those tears, for they are a language God understands." We should never be ashamed of godly emotion that the Holy Spirit has produced.

Why don't we ask the Holy Spirit today to help us pray? We don't need to work ourselves into some emotional state. We can just say, "Holy Spirit, show me what I should be praying for." He will lead us into prayer that produces wonderful results.

Holy Spirit, teach me to pray! I want to pray effectively and powerfully, as you want me to.

90

NO WORRIES

Don't worry about anything.

PHILIPPIANS 4:6

When the coronavirus pandemic broke out in 2020, the world experienced a disease out of control. So did the people of Europe, in the fourteenth century, when the Black Death wiped out an estimated one in three people. But there's another epidemic that's been around much longer that does more than just kill the body. It can affect the soul. It's called worry.

The same God who says, "Don't kill," and "Don't steal," also says, "Don't worry." Philippians 4:6 could be translated literally, "Don't worry about anything, not even a single thing." How many of us today are living in disobedience to God by worrying and aren't even aware of it?

Worry makes us more susceptible to disease. It also affects family relationships. When one person is consumed with worry and anxiety, it doesn't make for a happy meal around the table. Anxiety is destructive.

God is against worry because it falsely accuses him, as if we believe he's not going to take care of us. He gave his Son for us when we didn't know him. He sent the Holy Spirit. He gave us his Word. But we're still going to worry?

Imagine if when my daughter Sue was in the second grade, her teacher had called me and Carol in and said, "We've got a problem.

Your daughter's not learning like she should. She just stares out the window and bites her nails."

"What are you talking about?" we would have said.

"Well, I asked her what was making her so anxious, and she said, 'I'm worried that my parents won't pick me up after school.'"

Hearing that would have broken our hearts. We would have said to our daughter, "Sue, what do you mean? Have we ever not picked you up?"

"I know, but what if you stop doing it?"

Imagine how God feels when we worry.

Anxiety changes nothing about our situations. It only changes us physically, emotionally, and spiritually—and not for the better.

So here's the spiritual vaccine: "Don't worry about anything," little or big. "Instead, pray about everything. Tell God what you need, and thank him for all he has done" (Philippians 4:6).

The word *pray* signifies coming into God's presence and experiencing his love. We're to tell God our needs and petitions, laying out before him what's eating us up inside. But, the Bible says, we need to mingle it all with thanksgiving for what he's already done. We might have three problems today, but we've had 750,000 blessings over the years—the gift of God's Son being the biggest one of all.

And here's what the vaccine is guaranteed to do: "Then you will experience God's peace, which exceeds anything we can understand. His peace will guard your hearts and minds as you live in Christ Jesus" (Philippians 4:7). God's peace is not like ours. We have peace when things are going well. But when things go sideways? *Oops*, there goes our peace. God's peace, though, is unshakable. It's the peace that Jesus had. Whether he was walking on water, teaching, or standing in front of Pilate, nothing could rattle him. That's the peace God can give us today.

So let's not worry. Instead, let's bring God our petitions and leave them with him, like the old song says: "Take your burden to the Lord and leave it there."[19] When we do, God's peace will overcome anything that concerns us today.

Lord, by your grace, I am not going to worry today, because you love me and you will never fail me.

91

THE RIGHT WORDS

God will give you the right words at the right time.

MATTHEW 10:19

Jesus was sending his disciples out into dangerous, anti-God terrain. "You're going to be arrested and hauled before judges and governors," he told them. "But this will be an opportunity for you to bear witness for me" (see Matthew 10:16-18). Then he went on to say these amazing words: "Don't worry about how to respond or what to say. God will give you the right words at the right time. For it is not you who will be speaking—it will be the Spirit of your Father speaking through you" (Matthew 10:19-20).

In this day of widespread unbelief in the power of the Holy Spirit, this promise of Jesus is an eye-opener. Many Christians think that God speaking through us can't happen today. But it has to be able to happen, because we're constantly thrown into situations where we can witness for the Lord. When questioned about our faith, we can't always say, "Wait, let me go check some Bible commentaries and Greek word-study books. I'll get back to you." No. At that moment, the Holy Spirit will give us the words to say.

When Peter woke up on the Day of Pentecost, he didn't know that he would preach that day (see Acts 2). He had no notes prepared. But he knew what the Lord had promised: "When you're out there witnessing for me, thoughts, words, and boldness will be given you on the spot."

Many of us are silent about our faith because we worry, *What would I say? I don't know how to witness for Christ.* But the early followers of Jesus, who were young and full of flaws, held on to this promise throughout the history of the early church.

Back when I first went into ministry, one morning I got a premonition in prayer that a particular pastor in New Jersey was going to call me and say, "It's last minute, but would you come and speak for me tonight?" Sure enough, two hours later, that's exactly what happened.

I went, thinking, *Wow. If I ever knew I was supposed to be someplace, it's now.* But as the praise and worship started and I sat waiting to speak, suddenly the notes I had prepared went dead. All inspiration was completely gone.

So I started praying. "Oh, God, you sent me here. That I know. But, Lord, I have nothing." The praise and worship ended. The pastor gave the announcements. "God?" I was agitated, nervous.

Then I thought of Jesus' promise that he would give me the words I needed, when I needed them. So I prayed, "God, I have no idea what is going on here tonight, but I can only trust you." I can see myself even now, walking up the steps, across the stage. People were clapping. I had nothing.

But as the pastor handed me the microphone—*boom*—a light went on in my mind and my heart. God gave me a passage of Scripture, and I spoke, with no notes, for about half an hour. And it was the best sermon I had ever preached.

Today, we don't need to be anxious or worried about speaking for the Lord. Yes, we might be sent into difficult areas to speak for Christ. But the Holy Spirit will give us the words we need on the spot.

Lord, thank you that I don't need to be anxious when it comes to speaking for you. Give me words today to share you with others.

92

WHAT'S IN YOUR HEART?

It's not what goes into your body that defiles you.

MARK 7:15

I'm constantly around people who are following health fads. They drink tons of water. They don't eat fried or processed foods; they eat kale and salads and vegetables instead. If you order a Big Mac with fries, they look at you like you committed a felony. Healthy habits are definitely wise and helpful. But isn't it amazing that people who watch so carefully what they ingest physically, even many professing Christians, sometimes give very little thought to what's going on in their hearts?

The Jewish religious leaders in Jesus' day had an issue with this. These men had moved further and further from the meaning of Scripture, so that some of their rules were contrary to the Word of God. They noticed that the disciples didn't follow the Jewish ritual of ceremonial handwashing before they ate. So they complained to Jesus about it. But Jesus told the leaders, "You look spiritual on the outside, but your hearts are far from me! It's not what you eat that defiles you. It's what comes out of your hearts" (see Mark 7:9-15).

Later, when Jesus was alone with the disciples, they asked him about this. "Don't you understand either?" he replied. "Food doesn't go into your heart, but only passes through the stomach and then goes into the sewer" (Mark 7:18-19). No food defiles us spiritually before God. Why? It doesn't go into the heart. The heart is the all-important place, because "from within, out of a person's heart, come evil thoughts, sexual immorality, theft, murder. . . . They are what defile you" (Mark 7:20-23).

Shouldn't we give a lot more attention to the condition of our hearts than the condition of our bodies? No matter how much we take care of our bodies, we're going to die one day. My mother lived to 104, and she ate rather healthy her whole life, but she still died. What's in our hearts, however, affects us for eternity, and for believers, it affects our peace and joy in this world. We don't grieve the Spirit by eating a hot dog. We grieve the Spirit by harboring envy, slander, pride, or foolishness in our hearts.

So how do we find out what's in our hearts? When we go to a doctor, he or she can tell us how we are physically. But when we go to the Bible and get into God's presence, the Lord begins to show us what's going on in our hearts. That's why the psalmist said, "Search me, O God" (Psalm 139:23). Only the Lord can tell us what's going on inside us.

Country preacher Vance Havner, who was famous for his straight talk and pithy statements, wrote about riding a train through a town and seeing the beautiful fronts of all the homes kept up for appearance's sake. But in the towns where the train tracks ran behind the homes, he saw all the hidden junk. Maybe, Havner wrote, we need God to start cleaning up our back porches. We may look good to others, but what's going on in the back, where the junk is?

Let's ask God to show us what's in our hearts so we can live lives worthy of and pleasing to him.

God, put a searchlight on our hearts today,
and show us our heart condition.

93

BURNING WORDS

Didn't our hearts burn within us as he talked with us on the road?

LUKE 24:32

Two men were walking on the road to Emmaus. They were downcast and confused. The one they had thought would be the Messiah and bring deliverance to Israel had been beaten up, then crucified on a cross. Now their hopes were gone.

Suddenly Jesus, who had just risen from the dead, came and walked alongside them. He hid his identity, so they didn't know who he was. The Lord asked them, "What are you discussing so intently as you walk along?" (Luke 24:17).

As they told him about their disappointment and sadness, he said to them, "You are so foolish, and slow to believe the Old Testament prophecies!" Then Jesus took them through the Scriptures, explaining to them the things concerning himself (see Luke 24:25-27). They had the best teacher ever known to the world teaching them!

When they got to Emmaus, they asked him to stay with them. As they sat down to eat, Jesus "took the bread and blessed it. Then he broke it and gave it to them. Suddenly, their eyes were opened, and they recognized him" (Luke 24:30-31).

Then, with no warning, Jesus disappeared.

The men looked at each other. Then they exclaimed, "Didn't our hearts burn within us as he talked with us on the road and explained the Scriptures to us?" (Luke 24:32).

Understanding Scripture comes not just by reading it intellectually, like with every other book. It must come with revelation from the Holy Spirit. We need Jesus himself to teach us the Word. We've all had the experience of reading passages of Scripture over and over and then one day reading them again and saying, "Whoa, look at that! I never saw that before." That's the living Christ, through the Spirit, making the Scriptures alive to our hearts and applying them to our lives.

What we need today is Bible study that results in burning hearts touched by God. Every time we open the Scriptures, we should pray, "God, open your Word to my heart. Holy Spirit, teach me your will and ways" (see Psalm 119:18; John 14:26).

Second, we need pastors to preach in such a way that people won't be looking at their watches, thinking, "When can I get out of here?" Instead, we need Spirit-anointed sermons that produce burning hearts. When Peter, on the Day of Pentecost, preached a very simple sermon, people's hearts were stabbed within them, and they said, "Brothers, what should we do?" (Acts 2:37). It wasn't mere emotionalism. It was the Word made alive.

General William Booth founded the Salvation Army back in the 1800s with his wife, Catherine, who was herself a gifted speaker. Her sermon collections have been a blessing to me. Toward the end of her life, she said, "Burning words! That's what I'm looking for. I travel all around and I hear oratory; I hear clever preaching. But what I'm searching for is something that will burn my heart like the men on the road to Emmaus."[20]

Let's pray today that as we read the Word, our hearts will burn within us. And let's also pray for pastors everywhere, that when they speak, their sermons will be alive through the Spirit of God. May God's Word stir our hearts in such a way that carnal desires will be consumed and spiritual things will become foremost in our lives.

Oh, Lord, cause my heart to burn today as you open my eyes to what you want me to see in your Word.

94

THE HELPER WITHIN

I will ask the Father, and he will give you another helper.

JOHN 14:16, GW

Some days we feel helpless, bewildered, or crushed. We feel like help is out of reach. But the help we need is so much closer to us than we think. It's not far away in heaven. No, the helper lives within us.

Before Jesus went to the cross, he told his disciples that it was good for them that he was leaving. We can be sure that the disciples did not agree with that, because Jesus was everything to them. But the Lord told them, "Don't be afraid. I'm sending you another helper" (see John 14:16).

The Greek word for "helper," *paraklētos*, comes from two words. One is *para*, which means "alongside of." It gives the idea of being close by to guide and help. The word *paraklētos* is translated in many ways: helper, comforter, counselor, advocate. The Holy Spirit is very close to us. In fact, he lives inside us to guide, refresh, and encourage.

In a world where people are feeling helpless, we are not helpless. Jesus was everything his disciples needed. But now he's in heaven, and the Holy Spirit is our helper, comforter, and counselor. We are not alone.

It's sad that we sometimes think our help is far away in heaven when he actually lives inside us. I heard about a nineteen-year-old girl right here in Brooklyn who got overwhelmed by life and overdosed on her mother's prescription pills. She took enough to end her life. She felt that she just couldn't take it anymore.

Jesus sent us the Holy Spirit to help us. As a song our choir sings says, "With Jesus I can take it; with him I know I can stand."[21] We have the ever-present, intimate help of the Holy Spirit, who knows everything we're going through, and right now, today, offers us the compassion of God. He stands ready to help us, if we will just turn to him and call out to him, "Spirit, come and help me."

Sometimes, instead of looking to the Holy Spirit for help, we look to humans. But people fail us sooner or later. Then we can get bitter and cynical. Or we look to ourselves for help. But we end up letting ourselves down, which can cause depression and a sense of feeling overwhelmed. Jesus promised us the Holy Spirit to give us victory over those negative tendencies.

When Paul and Silas were beaten and put in a jail cell in Philippi, they sang at midnight (see Acts 16:22-25). How did they find the joy to sing in a situation like that? Forget the beating; we would be disgruntled just to be in a cell. A lot of us would say, "What's the sense of serving God if this is what happens?" But Paul and Silas had help from the inside—the helper Jesus had promised.

The Holy Spirit is working on our behalf today. Whatever we're going through now, let's avail ourselves of our resource in Christ—the helper promised by the Lord.

Thank you, Lord, for sending us another helper.
Help me to focus on you today, knowing that
you care and are closer than I can imagine.

95

WHAT PRAYER MEANS TO GOD

Your prayers and your acts of charity have ascended as a memorial offering before God.

ACTS 10:4, CSB

Cornelius stands out in the book of Acts as the one who brought about a new era of Christian missions. When Christianity began, it was thought of as an offshoot of Judaism. Jesus was Jewish; all the disciples were Jewish; Paul was Jewish. But through Cornelius—a Gentile—God unveiled the fact that the gospel was for everyone in the whole world.

Cornelius was a Roman soldier. But even though he was not a Jew, he "was a devout, God-fearing man, as was everyone in his household. He gave generously to the poor and prayed regularly to God" (Acts 10:2). What a staggering thought for us today—a non-born-again Gentile was searching after God. He was probably drawn to Judaism's monotheism versus the worship of thousands of gods in the Roman Pantheon.

But what's even more amazing is how God responded to this man's prayers. At three o'clock one afternoon, Cornelius had a vision of an angel. And the angel said to him, "Your prayers and your acts of charity have ascended as a memorial offering before God" (Acts 10:4, CSB).

So God arranged for Peter to come to Cornelius's house and give him the gospel. While Peter was preaching the gospel to Cornelius and his whole household, they all believed in the message. And then the Holy Spirit fell on the whole bunch of them, exactly like he had on the early believers in Acts 2.

Here we see something very special to God: a non-Christian's prayers and acts of kindness. God had heard and seen them, even though not one prayer of Cornelius was in the name of Jesus. Cornelius hadn't even known who Jesus was until Peter came and preached the gospel message to him and his family. How powerful prayer must be, that God noticed Cornelius's faithfulness in praying, praying, praying.

But think of this: Now God is *our* Father, and we come to him in the name of Jesus. How encouraging is that today? Won't our prayers be heard and seen by God, and our acts of kindness as well? If the Lord heard the prayers and saw the charitable acts of Cornelius, who was not even a believer, how much more will our prayers and kind deeds be honored by the Lord today?

Satan doesn't want any of us to believe that God answers prayer. But our Father God so treasures our prayers that he keeps them in bowls in heaven (see Revelation 5:8). And he tells us in the Bible that his house will be called "a house of prayer" (Mark 11:17), more even than a house of preaching or worship. As a Father, he loves it when his children come to him and say, "I can't handle this. Would you please help me, God?"

The best days in my life, no matter where I've been, have been days when I've spent time with the Lord praying. My worst days have been when I've skimmed through prayer and been busy with other things, even good things, that have drawn me away from being alone with God and laying out my needs before him.

The mightiest force on the earth is prayer, because whatever God can do, prayer can do, and prayer links us up with God.[22]

What an amazing thought, Lord, that you treasure my prayers in bowls in heaven. Teach me to pray like Cornelius did, seeking you with all my heart.

96

LET IT GO

Love . . . is not irritable.

1 CORINTHIANS 13:4-5

In 1 Corinthians 13, Paul described the "way of life that is best of all" (1 Corinthians 12:31). People can speak in the language of angels, he said, or have the gift of prophecy, or give everything they have to the poor, but if they don't love others, they are nothing (see 1 Corinthians 13:1-3). He was speaking about *agape* love—the divine love that both characterizes Jesus Christ and is the essence of our God.

Paul was writing to a church whose members were fighting and squabbling. This church excelled in the gifts of the Spirit, but in another way it was carnal because of its divisions and strife. One person said, "I follow Paul," while another said, "I follow Apollos." And then someone tried to one-up everybody else and said, "Well, I just follow Christ" (see 1 Corinthians 1:11-12). So Paul felt compelled to remind them about what's the best thing of all and how it behaves in everyday life: "Love is patient and kind. Love is not jealous or boastful or proud or rude. It does not demand its own way. It is not irritable" (1 Corinthians 13:4-5).

Wouldn't we all agree that one of the hardest things to bear in life is being with irritable people? They're moody. One day they're up; the next day they're down. They are so overly sensitive that almost anything irritates them. Carol and I once had a woman like this stay at our house for a few nights. Every morning when I came downstairs and saw her sitting in the living room, I knew that it would be another day of walking on eggshells. God can give us the grace to handle them, but touchy people are a trial to all of us.

Irritability is not a quality that's supposed to characterize the lives of people who belong to Jesus. But isn't that the way some of us are? We're shining sunbeams one day, and the next day it's dark clouds and thunderstorms. Irritable people, in their own sly way, seek to control every social situation. "You have to be careful how you walk and talk around me," touchy people silently communicate. "If you irritate me, I'll go off on you."

But often we don't look at irritability in ourselves as such a bad thing. "I'm having a bad day," we tell people. "I didn't get enough sleep." "You don't know what I'm going through."

Imagine if the disciples had come back from ministry and gone to Jesus with questions and needs, and he had said, "Would you leave me alone today? I've had it." Or what if we went to the throne of grace in prayer and, instead of finding open arms, we found that the Lord was in a bad mood? We would never know what day we could approach him. But Jesus never gets irritated.

When God's love fills us—that is, when Jesus controls us—we can have victory over irritability and touchiness. So let's ask God to give us that love in our hearts that will keep us patient and kind, even in unpleasant circumstances. There will always be temptations to become irritable, but through the Holy Spirit, we can overcome them one by one.

Oh, Lord, overcome any habit of irritability in me with your amazing love. Let your patience and kindness characterize my life.

97

KNOCKED DOWN BUT NOT OUT

We get knocked down, but we are not destroyed.

2 CORINTHIANS 4:9

As Christians in the Western world, we live rather pampered lives compared to many other believers around the globe. Others live in real danger just because they follow Jesus. Yet when things become a trifle difficult for us, we're often ready to complain and give up the fight of faith. The apostle Paul was just the opposite.

When he wrote to his beloved spiritual children in Corinth, Paul told them that his apostolic ministry of founding churches was not easy: "We have the light of the gospel in our hearts, but we ourselves are like fragile clay jars. We are pressed on every side by troubles" (see 2 Corinthians 4:7-8). Then Paul made it clear that his troubles didn't get the better of him: "We're afflicted in every way, but we are not crushed" (see 2 Corinthians 4:8).

For decades as a pastor, I've heard people say, "Why did that happen to me? It's not fair. Do you know what I'm going through?" Instead of exhibiting the power of God's grace working in jars of clay, they moan and groan and feel sorry that they're victims of circumstances.

Not the apostle Paul. He said, "Yes, I've been knocked down—but I've never been knocked out. I get back up." One of the characteristics of a great boxer is that when he gets knocked down, before the count of ten, he's back up and ready to keep fighting. Shouldn't we ask God for a little of that pugnacious spirit, by his grace? As jars of clay, we are vulnerable to all kinds of attacks. But the Holy Spirit can give us the ability, when we are knocked down, to get up again and to keep getting up.

So every time Satan tells us, "It's over," we can reply, "I resist you. It's not over. Although it doesn't look good and I'm hurting now and I have to dry tears from my eyes, it's not over until God says it's over." We all need that kind of spiritual fortitude.

In the locker room at the Naval Academy, I saw a sign that said, "When the going gets tough, the tough get going." At the hardest part of the basketball game, when the players are fatigued and the game is on the line, people who are tough get going. They're resilient.

The apostle Paul was the most resilient Christian who ever lived. He was a fragile jar of clay, just like the rest of us. But through the power of the Spirit, he didn't quit, and he encouraged others to follow his example. "We never give up," he wrote (2 Corinthians 4:16).

What kept him going? "Everything we're going through," Paul said, "is just light affliction compared to the incomparable weight of glory waiting for us when we see the Lord" (see 2 Corinthians 4:17). What we go through here and now is not even worthy to be compared with what's waiting for us in heaven.

Whatever we're facing today, we're going to get through it. We are going to make it. We will live and not die (see Psalm 118:17). We might get knocked down, but we won't be down for the count. God is going to help us. Let's get up and serve Jesus today.

Lord, sometimes I feel like Paul, with troubles on every side. But help me, when I'm knocked down, to get right back up. I know that tomorrow's reward will far outweigh today's difficulties.

98

LIVING WORTHY OF YOUR CALLING

Always be humble and gentle.

EPHESIANS 4:2

When I first entered the Naval Academy in Annapolis, Maryland, I was sworn in as a midshipman. With the other new cadets, I got my head shaved, learned how to wear a uniform, and was taught to shine my shoes. Our superiors told us, "Listen, you're a midshipman now. You're part of an elite group of young men. One day, you're going to be a leader, serving your country."

But that wasn't all. "When you go home on leave," they said, "you don't carry yourself as half Polish, half Ukrainian from Erasmus Hall High School in Brooklyn. No, no, no. That's gone. You're wearing the uniform of the United States Naval Academy now. You're special, and you've got to act special. You don't get in fistfights. You don't throw ketchup on an expensive steak." Yes, they actually taught us how to eat, along with a thousand other things. "Why? You're a midshipman."

When Paul was in prison for the cause of Christ, he wrote to the church in Ephesus, "I want you to walk worthy of the calling you've received" (see Ephesians 4:1). He was saying, "You're a Christian now. You're not a Republican or a Democrat. You're not white or black. Your first identity is as a Christian. Now walk worthy of your Lord."

The word *walk* in this instance means to order our behavior—to live on a daily basis in keeping with our calling. We don't become

Christians by works; we are saved by grace. But once we receive the gift of salvation, we've got to walk worthy of that calling.

So how do we know if we're walking worthily? Paul told us one way in Ephesians 4:2: "Always be humble and gentle."

We are to be humble. Always. The mark of a mature Christian, or a Christian whose roots have gone down deep with the Lord, is humility. Proud people, even if they could raise the dead or recite the New Testament, don't know the Lord very well. How do we know that? Because the first thing we realize about ourselves as we get close to the Lord is that we're nothing without him. Our righteousness is like filthy rags (see Isaiah 64:6).

This isn't negativity; it's the humility that must come so that Christ can fill us. Then we can say, "I can do everything through Christ, who gives me strength" (Philippians 4:13). Without this humbling, we can't walk in victory, because self and pride get in the way.

We're not just to be humble. We are also to be gentle. We are to be meek and careful in how we deal with others, even bearing with their faults. The Lord has borne with all our faults, so how can we jump down someone's throat for their failings?

This is why so many Christians who get involved in politics often lose their way. When a person is fighting culture wars, gentleness often goes out the window. But Christ never taught us to fight for him. He taught us to follow him.

A Christian without a spirit of humility and gentleness is a contradiction. How can we be proud and rough with people and then say that we're following Jesus, the Lamb of God? God resists the proud but gives grace to the humble (see James 4:6).

Let's walk worthy of our calling today. It starts by taking a low position.

Lord, humble me today so you can fill me with yourself. By your grace, I want to walk worthy of the calling of belonging to Jesus.

99

BREAKING THE CYCLE

Once again the Israelites did evil in the Lord's sight.

JUDGES 3:12

In the book of Judges, a similar kind of story is told over and over again. The names change, but the tale stays the same.

Here's the cycle: The Israelites drift into idolatry. God tries to get their attention, but they don't listen. They worship the gods of the people they have mostly conquered, in large part because they were greatly influenced through intermarriage. Then God, to chasten them, puts them under the heel of one of the neighboring nations, and for years they're ground into the dirt by people who use them as servants and control them. Then the Israelites finally cry out to the Lord, and God raises up a rescuer, a judge, to save them. So they have peace in the land for a number of years—until the cycle begins again.

We see this story in Judges 3, when the Israelites abandoned the Lord and worshiped idols. "Then the Lord burned with anger against Israel, and he turned them over to King Cushan-rishathaim of Aram-naharaim. And the Israelites served Cushan-rishathaim for eight years" (Judges 3:8). Finally, Israel cried out to the Lord for help, and the Lord raised up Othniel and gave him victory over their oppressors (see Judges 3:9-10).

So the Israelites were free under Othniel—but not for long. "Once again the Israelites did evil in the Lord's sight, and the Lord gave King

Eglon of Moab control over Israel because of their evil" (Judges 3:12). And they served Moab for eighteen years, and then they cried out to the Lord, and he raised up Ehud (see Judges 3:14-15).

Whenever the Israelites couldn't take it anymore, they cried out to the Lord. They knew the reality of what the psalmist wrote years later: "Call on me when you are in trouble, and I will rescue you" (Psalm 50:15).

But what the Israelites never learned is to stay devoted to the Lord. They were like people today who sincerely cry out to God in trouble when they realize that they can't get out of a mess. Yet when God delivers them and their prayer is answered, they soon go drifting away again, just to different idols, different circumstances—only to be chastened again and end up in another bind.

I've watched the pattern repeat itself many times over the years: "Pastor," people say, "we need a miracle." We pray; God answers. They're in church, proclaiming, "Let us testify. God has proven faithful!" But five months later, you can hardly find them. They're wrapped up with family or work. Then, three years down the road, when their marriage is falling apart, they come and say, "Please help us. We don't want a divorce. It will hurt the kids."

When we are desperate, it's good to remember that God answers prayer. But let's go further. God is calling us into fellowship with him, not pit stops at the gas station to fill up our tank, only to run out of fuel two hundred miles down the road. He wants us to walk with him—keep drawing close to him, abide in him, stay connected to him—so we can avoid the turmoil and pain that come from backsliding.

Let's not be up and down with God. Instead, let's pray the words of the old song, "Draw me nearer, nearer, blessed Lord."[23] Let's abide in Christ so we can grow into maturity.

Jesus, thank you for delivering me when I'm in trouble. But help me also to stay close to you, and to keep getting closer every day.

100

MORE FAITH

Your faith has made you well.

MARK 5:34

Jesus had just arrived in Capernaum, where crowds of people were waiting to bring him all kinds of problems. Jairus, the synagogue ruler, came to Jesus and said, "Would you please come to my house? My little daughter, twelve years old, is about to die. But if you come, she can be healed" (see Mark 5:23). Notice that he didn't have the faith to say, "She *will* be healed." But Jesus, in his gracious way, followed him.

In the crowd that day was a woman who had started hemorrhaging the same year Jairus's daughter had been born. She was ceremonially unclean, according to the Jewish teachings of the Old Testament. What she knew about Jesus, we're not sure. But she had a powerful faith in him. She was too shy to reach out to the Lord, but as the people jostled him, she said to herself, *If I can just sneak up behind him and touch the hem of his garment, I will be healed.* And so it was. She touched Jesus' robe, and she was instantly healed (see Mark 5:25-29).

In that moment, Jesus realized "that healing power had gone out from him." So he said, "Who touched my robe?" (Mark 5:30).

"What do you mean?" Jesus' disciples said. "Everyone's trying to get near you, sticking babies in front of you to bless them, and you say, 'Who touched me?'" (see Mark 5:31).

The woman, realizing she had been found out, fell trembling to her knees in front of Jesus and told him everything.

Notice what the Lord then said to this frightened woman: "Daughter, your faith has made you well" (Mark 5:34).

We might think Jesus should have said, "I made you well. The power came from me." But Jesus' power didn't go out to other people in the crowd. All kinds of people were touching and jostling him that day—and nothing happened to them. Yes, God has all power. But faith reaches out to receive the gift that God is offering.

It's the same as when people today go to church on a Sunday and get nothing out of it, while the person in the pew in front of them is saved or healed or receives a tremendous blessing from the Lord. Same pastor, same sermon, same building. But receiving from God is about faith.

God can be right next to us, offering us his unshakable promises, but it's only faith that connects us to the power of God. Peter said it this way: "Through your faith, God is protecting you by his power" (1 Peter 1:5).

Whatever we're facing today, let's pray, like the disciples did, "Increase our faith" (Luke 17:5). I wonder what the angels think, knowing as they do how much God loves us and wants to help us, when we're so full of unbelief that we struggle to believe that the sun will come up tomorrow.

Let's shake off our doubt and discouragement and begin to trust the Lord. That's a decision we can make. God has already made his decision—he loves us and wants to help us. Now do we want to trust him and receive? Let's say yes to him today.

Lord, give me more faith! I want to lay hold of your promises and believe that you will help me today—and every day to come.

Notes

1. Bill Gaither, "He Touched Me" (n.p.: Gaither Music Company, 1972).
2. Jim Cymbala, "My House Shall Be Called a House of Prayer" (Bill Gaither Praise Gathering, Indianapolis, Indiana, October 14, 1994), https://www.youtube.com/watch?v=U79YOKje2zU.
3. Hudson Taylor, "J. Hudson Taylor," GeorgeMuller.org, accessed May 29, 2024, https://www.georgemuller.org/hudson-taylor.html.
4. George Müller, "Soul Nourishment First," GeorgeMuller.org, May 9, 1841, https://www.georgemuller.org/devotional/soul-nourishment-first.
5. Annie S. Hawks, "I Need Thee Every Hour," *The Baptist Hymnal*, ed. William J. Reynolds (Nashville: Broadman Press, 1991), 85.
6. Samuel Rutherford, *Letters of Samuel Rutherford* (Carlisle, PA: Banner of Truth, 1997).
7. Don Moen, "Think about His Love," (Integrity's Hosanna Music, 1998).
8. Helen H. Lemmel, "Turn Your Eyes upon Jesus," *The Baptist Hymnal*, ed. William J. Reynolds (Nashville: Broadman Press, 1991), 243.
9. Larnelle Harris, "When Praise Demands a Sacrifice" *Larnelle Collector's Series*, Volume 1 (1988).
10. Andrew Murray, *Humility* (Fort Washington, PA: CLC Publications, 1997), 12.
11. Annie S. Hawks, "I Need Thee Every Hour."
12. *E. M. Bounds, Purpose in Prayer*, Christian.com, http://articles.ochristian.com/article10925.shtml. See also *Purpose in Prayer in The Complete Works of E. M. Bounds on Prayer*, foreword by Jim Cymbala (Ada, MI: Baker, 2004).
13. Jim Cymbala, *Fresh Wind, Fresh Fire* (Grand Rapids: Zondervan, 2018), chapter 1.
14. Unknown author, "When I Think of the Goodness of Jesus," *The New National Baptist Hymnal*, ed. C. E. Williams (Nashville: National Baptist Publishing Board, 2001), 138.
15. E. E. Hewitt, "More, More About Jesus," *The Baptist Hymnal*, ed. William J. Reynolds (Nashville: Broadman Press, 1991), 102.
16. G. Campbell Morgan, quoted in Dr. Paul Chappell, "In the Nick of Time," *Daily in the Word with Paul Chappell*, June 29, 2014, https://devo.paulchappell.com/in-the-nick-of-time.
17. Youth for Christ, which was begun in 1944, continues today to reach young people all over the globe with the message of Jesus Christ. See https://yfc.net/.
18. Carol Cymbala, "God Is Working," *He's Been Faithful*, Brooklyn Tabernacle Choir (New York: Brooklyn Tabernacle Music, 1999).
19. Charles A. Tindley, "Leave It There," *The New National Baptist Hymnal*, ed. C. E. Williams (Nashville: National Baptist Publishing Board, 2001), 142.
20. Catherine Booth, "Burning Words," He Is My Delight, November 24, 2017, https://heismydelight.com/2017/11/24/burning-words/.
21. Kirk Franklin, "My Life Is in His Hands," *The Rebirth of Kirk Franklin* (New York: GospoCentric, 2002).
22. Paraphrase of the quote by *E. M. Bounds, Purpose in Prayer*.
23. Fanny J. Crosby, "Draw Me Nearer," *The Baptist Hymnal*, ed. William J. Reynolds (Nashville: Broadman Press, 1991), 234.

About the Authors

Jim Cymbala has been the pastor of the Brooklyn Tabernacle for more than fifty years. His ministry is characterized by his emphasis on prayer in the church and dependence on the Holy Spirit for his leading and power. The bestselling author of *Fresh Wind, Fresh Fire* and *Fan the Flame*, he lives in New York City with his wife, Carol, who directs the Grammy Award–winning Brooklyn Tabernacle Choir.

Connect with Jim Cymbala

http://jesuseverydaybook.com

http://jimcymbala.org

 @PastorJimCymbala

 @jimcymbala

 @TheBrooklynTabernacle

Rebecca English Lawson has been helping ministry leaders write and publish their books since 2008. She is the general editor of *Living the Christ Life*, a one-year devotional of writings from classic Christian authors. Rebecca is director of communications at the Brooklyn Tabernacle and lives with her husband, Steven, in New York City.